'To all events around the world: You are only as relevant as the people who participate, their need you fulfil, and the experience you bring. Challenge the norm.'

—— **Make yourself matter!**

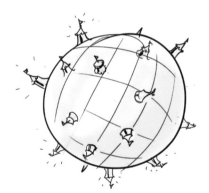

BIS PUBLISHING
Building Het Sieraad
Postjesweg 1
1057 DT Amsterdam
The Netherlands
T +31(0)20 515 02 30
bis@publishers.com
www.bis@publishers.com

Designer:
Cristel Lit
www.lots-of.nl

Editor and Contributing Co-Author:
John Loughlin

ISBN 978-90-6369-434-0
2nd printing 2018

EVENT DESIGN

handbook

Systematically design innovative
events using the Event Canvas

Roel Frissen | **Ruud Janssen** | **Dennis Luijer**

Co-contributors: David Bancroft-Turner | Dave Gray

B/SPUBLISHERS

YOU ARE ABOUT TO GO ON A RIDE!

ABOUT ME

Julius Solaris the editor of Event Manager Blog. Started in 2007, Event Manager Blog is the number one blog worldwide for event professionals, covering topics such as event planning, social media for events, event technology, event trends, event inspiration but also destination management marketing, meeting planning. He has been named one of 25 most inflluential individuals in the Meeting Industry in 2015 by Successful Meetings Magazine. He is the author of the Annual Event Trends Report, Social Media for Events, The Event App Bible , The Good Event Registration Guide and Engaging Events.

JULIUS SOLARIS
EDITOR OF EVENT MANAGER BLOG

I was attending an industry event a few days ago. The event planner of one of the most well known Business-to-Business events worldwide was speaking. The event in question is probably the go to, best practice reference in the industry.

I was struck by something that the speaker said: "We have no way of measuring the direct impact of this event in terms of sales. If you have a way to do it, I would love to see you afterwards". Wait, what?

One of the best events in Business-to-Business has no way to measure direct ROI? And the presentation actually started with the speaker saying how the main objective of the event was the bottom line!

'If you want to change behaviours,
you need to be ready to change yours.'

—— The way we create events is broken!

Many, many sources cite events as the go to tool for marketing, motivation and changing behaviours. When you look at your marketing mix for instance, events are constantly the most effective channel for brands. Yet the investment does not match the hype. The money put behind events is not as significant as the budget dedicated to other tools. Why is that?

If you work in events, like we do, I am sure you recognize the feeling that you are doing something amazing for the people around you, but you cannot quantify the impact or carefully measure the results. This is because the way we create events is broken. This is how important this book is.

In an industry where experience is preferred to education, we have let 'the way it's always been done' prevail over the 'why' we plan events in certain ways. The Event Design Handbook is shifting the focus of the conversation to what matters.

The authors have embarked in one of the most challenging tasks we have ever witnessed in the industry: changing the way we create events to offer better value for our attendees, partners, sponsors, bosses and for ourselves.

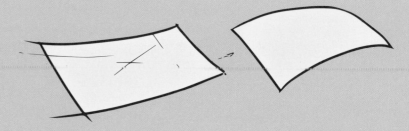

This book is aiming high, against biases, traditions and over a hundred years of doing things the same way. More than a manual, it is a manifesto of how events should be made. More than a process it is a philosophy. I see you there, dear reader, raising your eyebrows at the word 'philosophy' - 'what about practical things we need to do to make events better?' you may ask.

That is the unexpected twist of this immensely precious resource. Change needs to happen at a deeper level, challenging the status quo, but it also has to encompass simple steps and actions that you can take to make an impact. We, event professionals, love innovation but are very practical people. That's the merit of the authors. They are seasoned event professionals like you are. They are not taking you through self pleasing exercises, they are giving you a plan to action today.

This is not a book to read. This is a book to devour, to pass to your colleagues and boss. If you've ever felt frustrated with the way your company or organization does events, this book will be a relief. It will soothe that feeling you always had in the back of your mind when planning your event that most of the time ended up in frustration.

This book is also for the skeptical. It is for the seasoned event professional who has been tremendously successful in their career but is feeling the wind of change. For you, seasoned event professional, there is some good news and some bad news. The good news is that the authors got you covered. They know how your organization works, they know how your stakeholders think, they know how you make decisions. The bad news is

that you need to be ready to challenge the way you do things.
Eventually this will be the most beautiful takeaway from this journey.

What do you need to get started?

Before you embark in this adventure, get ready to analyze your behaviour,
challenge it and, if required, change it. Events are tools that through
education, networking and entertainment change behaviours.
If you want to change behaviours, you need to be ready to change yours.

The results will be amazing. I promise. So amazing that you will brag
about them to your friends and family. Yes, because planning events is
not about being obsessive compulsive with details. It is about hacking an
experience until you get the best possible result. It is about making even
the smallest element count toward a satisfied participant.

The Event Design Handbook will make history in our industry. It will
become the go to reference for making events better. It will be studied by
our children in universities, it will have a massive impact on the industry.

You are very fortunate, because you are the early adopter. You will gain an
incredible competitive advantage. In an industry where everybody fishes
in the same pond, you will have your own ocean of opportunities and it
will be so difficult for competitors to catch up.

So let's not waste any more time, let's get reading and make history
for the event industry.

THE STORY
OF THIS BOOK

This is Event Design—a uniquely powerful approach to systematically deconstruct and then reconstruct the success or failure of an event with a team of invested people. We have reduced the process of Event Design to one multi-faceted tool, fitting onto one piece of paper, that allows you to sketch all aspects of your event with your team. It is designed so that everyone can contribute, discuss, and debate the best possible way to design an event for its maximum possible impact. This tool is the Event Canvas™. Using it, you and your event team can make magic.

Did you judge this book by it's cover?

Well you're in for a surprise.

Like books, many events suffer from the syndrome of being judged by its cover. All pomp and circumstance from the outside and once you are in, you wonder what the fuss was all about. As a matter of fact, many events are like poor theatre plays, the ones where little thought is put into the script, casting and production and most don't even have a dress rehearsal. The truth is, this book has seen the daylight because it's time for a change. It's time to shake up the feathers and start an Event Design revolution.

Events are powerful mechanisms that change behaviour of its participants. You know they are, if you had the opportunity to participate in a properly designed event.

In this book we will share with you the power of the Event Canvas as a one page story. It will allow you to deconstruct that journey, articulate the mechanics of an event and then enable you to apply that to your future events together with your team.

As soon as you flip to the next page, you'll discover the power of visual thinking on a single piece of paper.

We have written this book in a casual style so you can easily consume its content, get inspired and share it with colleagues, friends and clients.

We've been tremendously inspired by seeing Event Design teams across the globe in action whilst we developed this Event Design methodology with them and can't wait to share these experiences and insights with you.

They have become Event Pioneers who are now having courageous conversations about value, using new tools that guide their fun collaborative processes. They are now equipped to design and articulate the true value of their events.

We are pleased and proud to welcome you to the Event Design handbook and the Event Canvas, so that you may systematically design innovative events. Let's design events for change, one event at a time,

Roel Frissen - Ruud Janssen - Dennis Luijer

Throughout this handbook you will run into this icon which indicates that there are additional resources available online as an extension to this book.
Look for them at www.eventcanvas.org/resources

NARRATIVE OF THE EVENT DESIGN HANDBOOK

You start the journey of reading this book eager to discover new ways of innovating events. You may have just discovered how Event Design offers that potential.

You are wondering how to inspire your team to join you on this journey whilst developing the ability to articulate how your events create value. These are the jobs you are trying to get done.

People in your environment are asking for innovations yet your event is actually pretty good already.

You bought the EVENT DESIGN handbook committing the time to read it. And heard that if you claim the right amount of event design time, space and mobilise the team you will be empowered to put your trust in them and the process of Event Design.

You expect this book to really help you get these jobs done at the cost of a lunch and a couple of cappuccinos.

As you get into the flow of the book you discover an Event Canvas with a visual language that enables you to get to the core of your event design as a team.

You discover how value is created through the CHANGE of behaviour of the relevant stakeholders, constrained by a design FRAME which ultimately prompts your team to come up with DESIGN prototypes. The most suitable of which you propose to your Event Owner.

You have landed yourself in a community of Event Design practitioners and their case studies inspire you to use your new tools and processes to discover how to contribute to the strategic conversation and get a seat at the table. It's you and your Event Design team that are setting the agenda and in the driver seat of delivering innovation to your organisation's future.

You are the Event Designers of the future, equipped, confident and having a blast designing with the end in mind. Get ready to discover and pass on your new insights to enable teams like yours to become just as successful as you have.

By handing them a copy of the EVENT DESIGN handbook.

IS THIS BOOK FOR ME?

CHAPTER 01

Presumably, your first reading of this book will be a solitary activity. Though it is full of illustrations, it is not at first glance the typical book you would gather people around to read together.

On the other hand, since this is a book specifically about bringing people together, both in events themselves and in the process of creating events, you may find yourself inspired to share much of this book with your colleagues. That is our intention. And if you find yourself gathering your team around to share passages directly out of this handbook or its online resources which are digital extensions of this handbook which are conveniently marked with the 🔗 as you read through the book, all the better.

Our approach is based on our experience, experiments, and expertise. The best results are garnered from bringing people together in an event, or from collaborating in the design of an event. They do not come from focussing on the logistics of an event, but rather from focussing on the abstract needs of everyone involved.—to be empathic. The problem: in current business environments, it's a slippery prospect to hold meetings, make plans, or convince others based on abstractions, like your empathy for the feelings of others. How do you structure empathy? How do you quantify people's needs—people you haven't met—people who themselves may not even know their particular needs?

Well, to support the empathic approach in designing events, we have created a tool to do just that: make concrete the abstract. It's called the Event Canvas, and it's the core of this book. We are Event Designers who train and consult Executives and Event teams. Our fascination for events and how they matter to us as human beings is the raison d'être of this book. This is not a book about how to best meeting-plan the perfectly executed event, but how to understand the human elements inherent in any event so that you can design better and more effective events.

We train teams to apply the methodology to elevate the field of Event Design and we advise clients from membership based organizations to NGOs and corporations. Throughout this publication you will see that we capitalize Event Design; we do so specifically to demonstrate our belief that the field is worthy of long-overdue respectability. We have devised the Event Canvas as a tool to facilitate clear collaboration and promote thinking visually in the process of creating tailored events. We have found that using the Event Canvas helps designers deconstruct the way events create value for participants and design team members alike. Together we will explore the mechanics involved in inspired Event Design.

EVENTS

When we talk about events in this context, we mean something specific, and broad. We define events as having two clear attributes. An event is a gathering of two or more people, or groups of people. Your reading this book on your own doesn't count as an event, but when you call a meeting to include others and share ideas from this book, that might be an event.

Events also require that the people involved have something at stake. They choose to create or be part of an event because it is more important to be involved than it is to not. As such, an event can be considered as any gathering that you would put into your schedule: squash with the boss after work; the 50th anniversary barbeque on Saturday; taking clients out next Tuesday; the conference call in the morning; drinks with the new hire; the week-long annual international ornithology conference in Tokyo next month. If it's in your agenda and there's someone else involved, it's an Event.

STAKES

Sometimes the stakes in an event are low, other times they can be extremely high. We know one thing for sure: every participant enters the event one way and walks out of the event affected somehow, hopefully for the better (and hopefully by your design). This is the first aspect to analyse in designing a quality event: the change that comes over a person after having experienced an event.

We symbolise that change by using a visual metaphor, the Event Tent. The circus tent represents the space into which a person enters as predictably herself, but then from which re-emerges as someone new, affected. And it is this space, and therefore the change it engenders, that we as event designers are tasked to manage to the greatest effect.

Can you remember the anticipation of going to the circus as a child? You saw the circus come to town. You saw the circus tent going up. You got your tickets.

And finally the magical day arrived and you went to the circus. Going into the tent brought you to an experience and set of emotions that elicited a change in you. Your behaviour coming out was different than your behaviour going in.

Going in, part of your anticipation arises from your innate ability to register such change in others. Remember your friends who went to the circus before you and how they were excited? Even if you didn't know exactly what went on inside the tent, you could see the change it created in them. What magic must have happened in there?

This book will show you how to deconstruct that transition (in yourself and in others), show you how to articulate the mechanics of an event in regard to that change, and then enable you to apply this knowledge to your future events.

Do you feel that everyone wants to be innovative, but no one knows what that looks like?

IS YOUR TEAM NOT ON THE SAME PAGE?

ARE YOU DONE WITH EXTENSIVE REPORTS AND WANT A ONE PAGE PLAN?

DO YOU WANT YOUR TEAM TO BE INVOLVED IN DESIGNING AN EVENT?

Are you trying to come to grips with the process of how events create value?

Do you wish you could design the outcomes of your event?

Do you long to lead your team to come up with solutions that will make them proud?

ARE YOU REPEATING THE MOTIONS OF DELIVERING EVENTS AND DREAMING OF WAYS TO INNOVATE?

DO YOU NEED TO BUILD A BUSINESS CASE FOR YOUR FUTURE EVENT?

DO YOU KNOW, OR HAVE YOU EXPERIENCED, THAT EVENTS CAN CREATE FUNDAMENTAL CHANGE?

IS THIS BOOK FOR
YOU?

If any of these questions or conditions resonate with you, then this book is for you. The Event Canvas is a tool flexible enough that it will prove useful to the student and the teacher; to the veteran event planner, the innovator, and the novice; to teams and individuals; to CEOs, event owners, team leaders, and interns alike. It is designed to elevate the experience of any participant, to promote the conscientious design of events, to allow you to articulate the story of your event, and to bring your team together. This book is for you, and for them. It is your team's compass.

This is a book to be shared.

SHARE

Share your questions, pictures and user generated content by using the hashtag #EventCanvas, which is used by your fellow readers and Event Canvas practitioners across the world.

CHANGE, BEFORE YOU HAVE TO

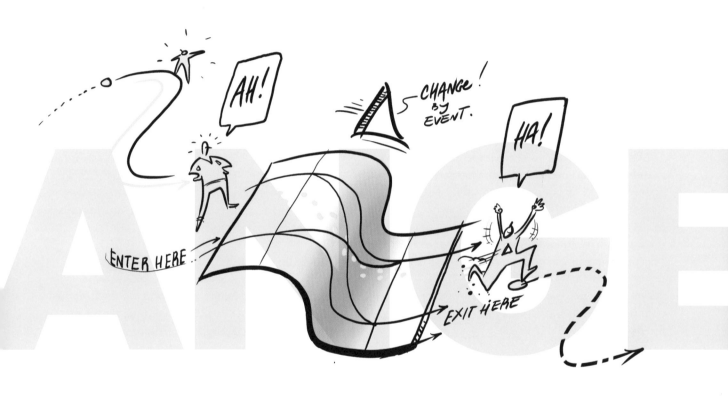

CHAPTER 02

23

CHANGE; INCLUDING YOUR OWN

The event industry as we know it today is occupied by a committed and traditional field of experts who are mainly focused on continuity and value. They ensure stability by building on relationships practices that in the past helped launch previous events. The events themselves have become businesses. But in order for event planners to survive in today's growing experience market they need to evolve. There is a tested and proven better way to design events that includes quantifying the abstract, empathizing, and planning for change.

Whether you are a CEO, the owner of an event, or a designer, in employing the methods we describe, you, too will make a change for the better—in your practice, in your results, and in your career.

Many of the advancements you make will be individual, but we can identify a few aspects that will be innovative to many. First, the Event Canvas is a visual tool. Creating a visual overview will ensure a transparent process that is easy to share and allows you to involve, include, or inform others by simply taking them through a clear visual process. Thinking visually allows people to gather around a problem and to constructively build a shared model for a complex idea. The Event Canvas uses a specific visual process that gives you direction by cutting the process into different modules, helping you to ask the right questions at the right time and exposing the insights needed to make conscious choices.

Second, you will be able to identify and articulate what is commonly elusive to most, and therefore neglected. Event planners often focus on the logistics and execution of an event, because these are quantifiable, but will neglect what we believe to be essential: the subjective experience, the abstraction of behaviour, and the journey of behaviour change. These seem to be unquantifiable, that they are not able to be evaluated and addressed. This is a mistake and the Event Canvas will change that perspective. With it you can map the needs of people participating in your event, their desires, and their expectations. It is a tool that will allow you to put into words the shared change you want to realize with your event.

And third, the Event Canvas is a unifying tool. It will keep a team focused, together, and on a track that leads through each and every consideration necessary in designing an excellent event.

'The ultimate value of an event is realizing change. It takes aligning with multiple perspective to be able to do so.

—— **Change requires empathy**

EMPATHY

Throughout the Event Design process, the challenge is to be empathetic. A key ability in being successful in Event Design is to see and dissect the different experiences and outlooks of a variety of strangers, and also to anticipate and influence how a single individual changes his or her perspective over the course of an event. The focus is on the person, and not the logistics and execution. This is user-centric design.

User-centric design is gaining in popularity, but it is harder to put into practice than it sounds. A person naturally designs from his or her own perspective. The Event Canvas and it's supporting tools are designed to make user-centric design possible. The Empathy Map (which we analyse in detail in chapter 5, where we interview its creator Dave Gray), and an alignment tool and the LEAD model (both of which we explore in chapter 7 with David Bancroft-Turner who is a true expert in the field) all offer precise ways to manage things as seemingly imprecise as change, empathy, behaviour, and influence. There is no other tool that fits them together with an iterative process in a template tailored specifically for Event Design except the Event Canvas.

LEADERSHIP-EXPERIENCE GRAPH

Your first step in analysing perspectives is to identify your own. Examine where you stand in the event design field, and in a particular project, by placing yourself on the Leadership-Experience graph.

Where do you land on the graph? What about the rest of your team?

Also use this graph to identify your aspirations. What is the change in perspective you strive to achieve? What is the level of responsibility you hope to attain? What about your level of expertise? Chart your target and your progress over the course of your career.

BRAIDING POINT

Next, be clear about when in the process you and your team are being asked to join the development of the event. We call this the braiding point. You are joining the process in essential and intertwining ways, but some threads most likely have been in place long before your involvement. It is important for you to be clear about your braiding point to keep old and new ideas in perspective. Where is the event owner coming from and what does the event mean to her interests?

It is important to identify the perspectives already in place.

This self-reflection is useful in gaining clarity on your own role and perspective. But it also acts as a good warm-up empathy exercise before you assess the multiple perspectives of the many parties interested in the event you design.

TWO BASIC PRINCIPLES

And so, after dissecting your position, role, and perspective, and that of your team, it will be useful to remember a couple of Basic Principles. Use them as touchstones while you begin to analyse the multiple and evolving perspectives of others. We'll explore both of these principles more later, but here's a quick introduction.

BASIC PRINCIPLE I

Events create value by changing the behaviour of its Stakeholders.

To track that change, we will have to articulate the behaviours that people have prior to the event, and analyse what their behaviours are likely to be after having participated in the event. We will study this in detail promptly in the Empathy Map sections.

BASIC PRINCIPLE II
It takes at least 2 Stakeholders to create an event.

Because, by definition, there is more than one person in an event, there is also more than one perspective. And also, by definition, the participants have a stake in the event. Therefore, we call any person who makes an event an event, 'Stakeholder'. Every Stakeholder comes with her own story, background, expectations, and trajectory. The essence of the Event Canvas is to analyse thoroughly each Stakeholder's perspective, whether it be that of a vendor, a participant, a keynote speaker, or whomever. The Event Canvas charts the process of identifying with multiple Stakeholders.

ANTHONY L. BACK, MD
PROFESSOR, DIVISION OF ONCOLOGY,
UNIVERSITY OF WASHINGTON MEDICAL CENTER

'The Event Canvas is incredibly useful for designing conferences that will make a difference – it brings together a great deal of wisdom into a practical workspace!'

LET'S LOOK
AT SOME REAL STAKEHOLDERS

Throughout the text you will meet Event Canvas users and learn about their perspectives. As you read about these people, imagine where they'd fall in the Leadership-Experience graph.

Here's Anthony Back. He's one of the early adopters of the Event Canvas and has used it design an event for one of his projects.

Scattered through the rest of the book you will connect to other users like Anthony. We'll meet an event manager for a management consulting firm, a Chief of Staff of a university, a Secretary General for a risk management federation, the head of events for the International Olympic Committee and many others.

Even though these people have different experiences, and their stakes are all different, the one thing they have in common is that they use the Event Canvas. The Event Canvas can help you, too, get to where you want to be with an event, with a team, and with your own career path across the Leadership-Experience graph. So, next meet Marti Winer and then let's examine the Event Canvas in detail in Chapter 3.

The Cam

MARTI WINER

CHIEF OF STAFF DREW UNIVERSITY – ACADEMIC

"Each time you plan to start a business, launch a product, market to a new audience, or engage in an array of other activities, your first step is to build a business model, isn't it? Of course it is.

It would seem crazy to embark on the execution of a strategy before you have written it. Why is hosting an event any different? When you decide to host an event, regardless of who the attendees are, you need a plan. Otherwise how would you know who is involved, why you are hosting, and what you are hoping to achieve. You probably know these answers in your head, the way you envision business strategy before you even write it down, but can you articulate it for those tasked with planning your meeting? You might think so, but do they? If you have ever shown up at an event and felt that it fell flat or failed to meet your expectations, it might be that you weren't speaking the same language.

ABOUT ME

Holding various positions within the hospitality, marketing, real estate and financial services industries throughout her accomplished career, Marti Winer worked for Wyndham Hotel Group, the world's largest hotel company as their vice president of Global Communications and Event Services. Her team executed 50 events and more than 100 trade shows internationally each year. In 2014, Marti left Wyndham to become Chief of Staff at Drew University handling the operations of the university, as well as generating auxiliary revenue in an academic environment.

'I found it to be a helpful tool in organizing our thoughts and ideas for our event.'

—— It allowed us to articulate the 'story'

So often your vision and intent gets lost in translation. Alternatively, there are often several stakeholders in an event and with so many directions coming from different sources, the message gets muddled and no one leaves the event with clarity.

That is where an Event Canvas comes in. With an easy-to-use tool and a simple process to follow, you can fill in the gaps between your thoughts and the execution of your event making ambiguity all but disappear. Either using it to facilitate a team discussion or to gut-check your own vision, the Event Canvas streamlines input allowing you to articulate the role of each stakeholder and to gain alignment before anyone starts to plan a thing. Just like a business model…but tailored to suit the business of live events."

03.

"INTRODUCING THE TOOL" . AHA!
AH! HA!

MEET THE
EVENT CANVAS

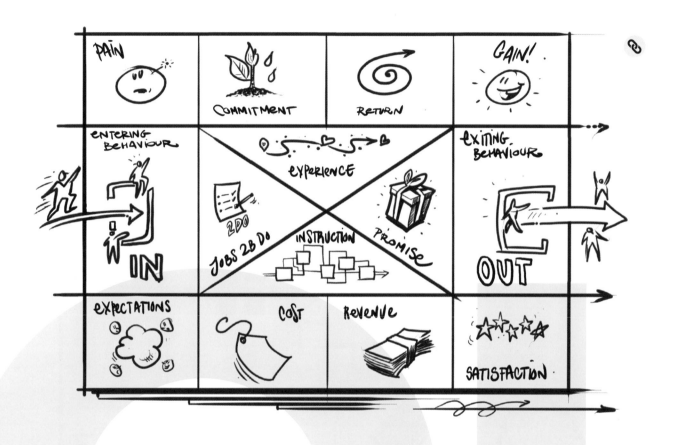

Now that you've gotten a general sense of what the Event Canvas™ can do by learning it's intended usefulness, by seeing who it is for, and by hearing from people who have used it (which will continue throughout the book), it's time to take a closer look at the tool itself and its specific parts. Simply put, the Event Canvas is a template to support Event Design.

An event is one of the most powerful instruments for influencing the behaviour of the people who attend.

In that respect the Event Canvas is a template for designing the way that a person exiting an event takes action, based on what he or she experienced and learned.

In the following chapter, we'll explain in much greater detail the process of applying the Event Canvas for your project. But for now, we are just creating definitions. Let's first examine, in general, how it is applied in the Event Design process.

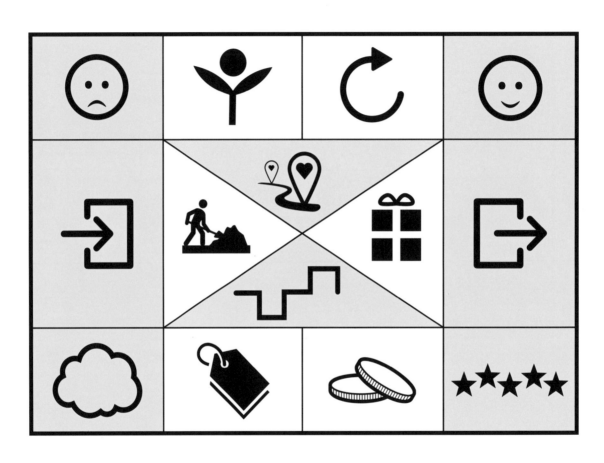

 www.eventcanvas.org/resources

TEAM PROCESS

Working with the Event Canvas is a shared team process that promotes contributions from each member, and in so doing, helps the team come up with multiple possible design options and then choose which will best change the behaviours of the key Stakeholders.

To work with the Event Canvas, the team works together in a dedicated space. The team creates a list of Stakeholders, then a Canvas for each Stakeholder, and then fills in each Event Canvas in a systematic, collaborative way.

FOR STAKEHOLDERS...

The Event Canvas is the embodiment of a Stakeholder's perspective. To understand its parts, it is critical to keep this in mind. We often hear questions like, 'What are the objectives of the event?' The answer must be that, in truth, an event itself does not have objectives. Stakeholders in an event are the ones who have objectives. This might seem a semantic quibbling, but keeping this clear is fundamental to maintaining the correct perspective throughout the Event Design process.

Different Stakeholders have different stakes in, and different objectives for, an event, and so each needs his or her own Canvas. The Event Canvas visualises the different stakes that various Stakeholders have in an event, and then allows you to design for their behaviour change.

...AND THEIR CHANGE IN BEHAVIOUR

Successful events are designed to change behaviour. The basic purpose of the Event Canvas is to identify the stakes of Stakeholders and to track and predict how those stakes are addressed, affected, influenced, and map how they are changed as a result of the event. This change in their stakes will be most evident in the Stakeholder's behaviour, and in how it changes from before the event to after the event. And it is this change in one Stakeholder's behaviour that may very well be the stake of another Stakeholder. We consider it the purpose of Event Design to create events that change people's behaviour and generate new trajectories for everyone involved. Really, why else have an event?

In order to visualise behaviour change, describe the current behaviour of the Stakeholder before the event and the desired behaviour after the event. The Event Canvas helps you to do just that by mapping the stakes, then making the frame, and then designing the change. CHANGE-FRAME-DESIGN. This is embodied in the layout of the Event Canvas, so let's look at that layout.

THE LAYOUT

14 BLOCKS

The Event Canvas is a rectangular paper template filled with 14 discrete building blocks: 10 rectangular boxes of various sizes around the perimeter; and within that perimeter, a box divided into 4 triangles by two diagonal lines crossing in an X pattern. We'll go over each of these blocks one at a time in this chapter to give you an understanding of what each one is for, and then in later chapters see examples of real-world applications of the individual boxes and how they work together.

3 PHASES, CHANGE-FRAME-DESIGN

To go over each block, it is important to first divide the Canvas into 3 groups of blocks so that we can identify interactions within the Event Canvas and suggest an order to the process. These phases are called CHANGE, FRAME, and DESIGN.

CHANGE

The first group of related blocks is called CHANGE, here represented by the 6 blue blocks on the far left and the far right of the template. CHANGE represents the way Stakeholders enter an event (on the left) and exit an event (on the right).

FRAME

Six other blocks make up the FRAME. These blocks are represented in green in our graphic and command the majority of the central column of blocks: Two rectangles on the centre-top, two rectangles on the centre-bottom, and the left and right triangles in the middle. These blocks define a boundary area, or frame, within the Event Canvas that is necessary to focus exactly what it is that you are designing.

DESIGN

The DESIGN region of the Event Canvas is made up of only two blocks: the top triangle and the bottom triangle in the very centre of the Canvas. They are coloured in sea green in our graphic and make an 'hourglass' shape. They represent two ways of learning—by experience and by instruction—and together they represent the actual event. It is this part of the process that will deliver how the event will actually look and feel.

These three parts together form an alliance. CHANGE–FRAME–DESIGN represents a logical breakdown of the three steps in the process of Event Design and allow us to dig deeper into the Event Canvas template.

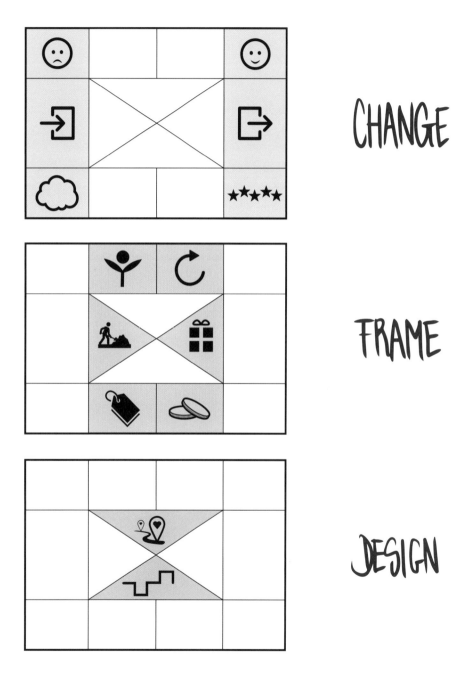

CHANGE

FRAME

DESIGN

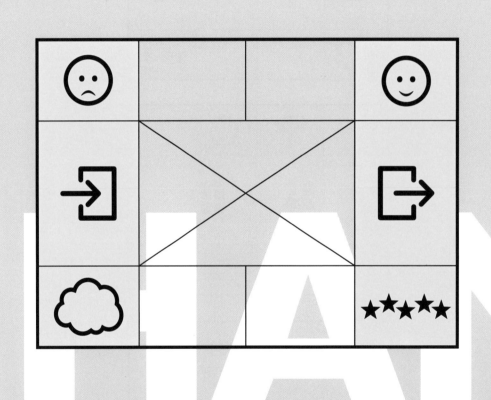

CHANGE

ARTICULATING THE CHANGE IN BEHAVIOUR

THE STORY OF THIS EVENT

Consider an example of this event with 5 Stakeholders: Lee is a photographer who works freelance. His friends are all in media arts—photographers, videographers, writers, painters—and they all also work freelance. They've each had one or two jobs with big-time media outlets—Italian Vogue, the New York Times—but would like more consistent client interest. Lee is going to host a Saturday barbeque and invite his media arts friends and their highest level contacts from their recent jobs. Lee expects 40 to 50 people and has secured a popular brunch location with a big outside area. He has a sponsor:

a camera manufacturer is donating a free version of its photo-editing software through a raffle and sending two of its employees.

The 5 Stakeholders are Lee, as the event owner, his media arts friends, the media outlet representatives, the camera corporation, and the restaurant.

Let's begin with the CHANGE group, which charts the most important measure of an event: Behaviour Change.

01 ENTERING BEHAVIOUR

In this box we consider Stakeholders before they experience the event. This is important to stress. ENTERING BEHAVIOUR is not the behaviour of a Stakeholder walking into an event. It is their behaviour completely independent of the event, how they are and who they are in their ordinary lives even if you don't have your event.

First, we have to define the various types of Stakeholders that will be involved. There must be an event owner, and participants. Are there guests, presenters, sponsors? For each Stakeholder group that we identify, we will create an Event Canvas, and start right here to fill in ENTERING BEHAVIOUR.

Describing the behaviour of a Stakeholder can be challenging because every human being is unique. There are thousands of behaviours we might expect at an event, and thousands of books about behaviour we might consult to get a handle on the task of describing behaviour, which makes mastering it very daunting.

We like to generalise it by saying that it is everything you might observe of a person through a camera. Additionally, we are not looking to describe every individual behaviour; we are looking for instances

QUESTIONS TO ASK

Before this event imagine characteristics of such a representative:
1 How would you describe his/her current behaviour?
2 What are his/her present skills, knowledge level, attitude, connections?
3 What does he/she say and do?
4 What is his/her behaviour towards others? What is his/her attitude in public?
5 How would you describe his/her appearance?

of commonality in the behaviours within Stakeholder groups. It helps to visualise a representative of the group when describing behaviour; use personas for Stakeholder groups.

Let's consider a few examples of ENTERING BEHAVIOUR. The owner, Lee, is somewhat new in town and has been successful finding freelancers in similar straits, but not clients. He is frustrated and unsure how to make inroads. The artists are a mix of frustrated, complacent, and resigned that the life of the artist is to always be unrecognised and

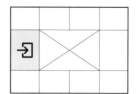

underfunded. The media companies seek new trends and talent. The restaurant is torn about private parties: guaranteed money and exposure, but limited bill and presentation. The camera company is struggling to be respected in the photo-journalism community and has spent resources to develop tools to legitimise itself, including an image-editing platform.

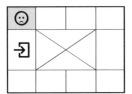

PAINS 02

1 What are his/her fears, frustrations, obstacles?
2 What makes him/her feel bad?
3 What really worries them?
4 What keeps them up at night?

When we talk about pain in everyday life we refer most often to physical, or sometimes mental, anguish. This is not the PAIN we address here. When we talk about PAINS, we mean thoughts and feelings that keep people from doing something, personal circumstances that block change and that preserve the status quo. This includes anything that annoys the Stakeholder in his daily life, undesired costs and situations, negative emotions, and risks.

Some PAINS are severe and others are light. Some can be superficial and sometimes very deep. Lee's PAINS might be the social discomfort of mixing friends and business, needing to appear trend-setting, and losing friend-time to hustling for jobs.

Understanding these PAINS is important because, first of all, they are important to the Stakeholder, on a conscious or subconscious level, and second because if the event can alleviate the PAIN, this Stakeholder will be fully receptive.

03 EXPECTATIONS

This one is almost self-explanatory. You and your team simply consider the EXPECTATIONS a Stakeholder might have before coming to an event. Keep in mind that EXPECTATIONS are subjective, and often subconscious. When we receive and process new information, we build and adjust their EXPECTATIONS continuously. The artists might have the EXPECTATION that socializing with corporate media representatives will feel insincere.

EXPECTATIONS are interpretations of information from outside sources, such as:

1 **A previous experience**—how a Stakeholder experienced a prior event.
2 **Word-of-mouth**—what others tell the Stakeholder about the event, about their own experiences, or about what they have heard from others.
3 **Social media**—what is broadcast and discussed online.
4 **Marketing messages**—the information provided by the event organiser.

These EXPECTATIONS are a crucial part of the mind-set a Stakeholder has going into an event. This is very valuable information for the design of the event. And if you wish to meet, or exceed, those EXPECTATIONS, you can only do so by getting to know what they are.

QUESTIONS TO ASK

1 What are his expectations, based on previous experiences? Previous events he attended? Previous editions of this event?
2 What do others say about this event?
3 What is said on social media about the event?
4 What does he learn from the marketing messages he receives from the event?

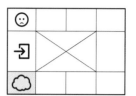

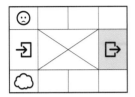

EXITING BEHAVIOUR

QUESTIONS TO ASK

1   As a result of this event, what new skill, knowledge, attitude, or connection has he/she acquired?
2   What is his/her attitude in public?
3   How would you describe his/her appearance?
4   What does he/she say and do differently?

The first step in changing the behaviour of Stakeholders is to determine their patterns of behaviour before the event (BLOCK 01). The next step is to describe the desired behaviour. Ask yourself, 'How do I want this Stakeholder to leave the event?' Next, visualise the answer to the comparison question, 'How is he or she likely to behave as a result of having participated in this event?' How is this EXITING BEHAVIOUR different than before the event?

Remember, behaviour is a combination of what a person says and does and is delineated as everything you can observe through a camera. Consider what the Stakeholder has learned—what new skill, knowledge, attitude, and connection the Stakeholder has acquired during their experience of the event.

GAINS

In direct response to PAINS, GAINS describe the positive outcomes and the benefits for the Stakeholder—what he or she requires, expects, desires, or might even be surprised by—such as functional utilities, social gains, positive emotions, and cost savings. Some outcomes and benefits will be more tangible than others.

If Lee's PAIN is the awkwardness of mixing friends and business, his ideal GAIN might be in seeing his friends socialise gracefully with industry people, and even the two camera sales reps are chatting easily with strangers. (Such relief!—that's GAIN: PAIN alleviated.)

Mapping GAINS gives you insight into the motives of Stakeholders. Creating GAINS for Stakeholders engages them more intimately in the event and what it offers.

QUESTIONS TO ASK

1   What does this Stakeholder want, need, or dream of?
2   What does he or she desperately want to have?
3   What benefits is he/she seeking?

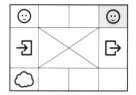

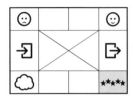

SATISFACTION 06

1   What is the subjective interpretation of the experience the event offered?
2   What does he/she tell friends, family, colleagues about the event?
3   How would he/she qualify this experience?
4   What will Stakeholder communicate on social media after the event?
5   How does he or she assess the experience compared to other experiences?
6   How does the experience influence the decision making about future experiences?

EXPECTATIONS are a crucial part of how, and with what mind-set, someone will start his or her journey. It's 'after' counterpart, SATISFACTION, is the result of that journey. The artists' SATISFACTION might be, Media company representatives are creative and interesting, after all; it's more fun to connect with them than I expected.

A rule of thumb about SATISFACTION: 'Many more people tell others about bad service than they do about good service.'

Of course, we'd like to meet, and occasionally exceed EXPECTATIONS, to deliver experiences of SATISFACTION beyond what Stakeholders expected. This can only be accomplished when EXPECTATIONS and SATISFACTION have been charted in the Event Canvas.

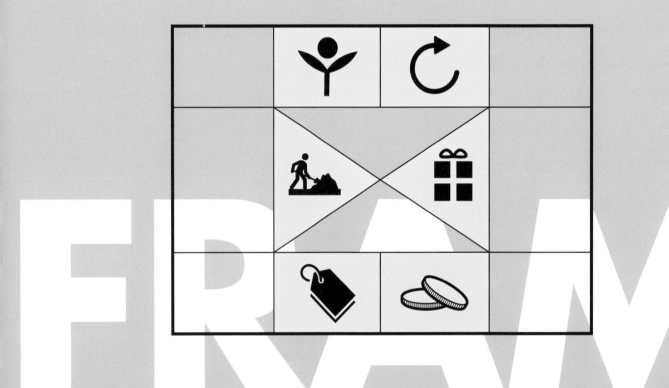

FRAME

DEFINING THE DESIGN BOUNDARIES

If CHANGE charts details before the event and after the event, FRAME is what happens in between: the event itself. FRAME is the boundary box of practical realities within which you need to contain your event. It is therefore placed in the middle of the Canvas, between the ENTRY blocks and the EXIT blocks. Design is a process that is guided by a goal, a strategy, and boundaries. In order to start the Event Design process properly, we need to design the FRAME. The design requirements that define the project describe the reality and limitations of the event and help to bring focus to the design. Without a FRAME the design process would go on indefinitely and would be called art.

The FRAME in the Event Canvas consist of 6 blocks dominating the middle trunk of the template:

COMMITMENT, RETURN, COSTS, REVENUES, JOBS TO BE DONE, and the pivotal PROMISE to the Stakeholders.

These blocks form the constraints in which the Event Design must deliver its intended value. Once this boundary box has been defined, the creative challenge to do the actual design has now been set.
The top blocks COMMITMENT and RETURN, and bottom blocks COST and REVENUE are mirrors of each other: the top blocks are the 'soft' ideas—emotionally-driven: whereas the bottom blocks are hard currency—quantifiable in terms of money, contacts, or contracts. And these two rows carry the left-to-right chronology. Stakeholders come in with COMMITMENTS and COSTS, and leave with and RETURNS and REVENUES.

07 COMMITMENT

Having a stake in an event always involves some level of commitment. With COMMITMENT we aim to raise our understanding of the Stakeholders' personal investment to either initiate, attend, partner in, or sponsor the event. A COMMITMENT often means that the Stakeholder is sacrificing something in order to commit.

COMMITMENT is often expressed in time, energy, or time away from the office or the family. Also, the reservation or use of resources, preparation, and efforts of different kinds are examples of commitment. The artist's COMMITMENT might be, I'm giving up a Saturday for this.

Understanding these trade-offs, compromises, and opportunity costs the Stakeholder faces will provide us insight into how to create a positive experience and also helps to exceed EXPECTATIONS.

QUESTIONS TO ASK

1   What is the non-monetary investment the Stakeholder makes, whether tangible or intangible?
2   What sacrifice is he/she expected to make to attend this event (time, compromise, opportunity cost)?
3   What does he/she choose not to do or attend because of this event?

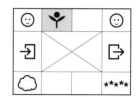

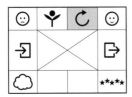

RETURN

QUESTIONS TO ASK

1 What does he/she walk away with after the event?
2 What would he/she expect in return for going to this event?

When committing to an event as a result of having a stake in it, the Stakeholder needs some sort of return on his COMMITMENT: his trade-offs, compromises, and opportunity costs. RETURNS are important in delivering gratification to the Stakeholder in the most streamlined way. Whereas GAINS concern the long term results, RETURNS are focused on the short term output of the event.

RETURNS can be tangible or intangible, for example: I ate well, had some good chats, saw some old friends, and put my name on the radar of big-time publishers without having to feel forced or sending out portfolios or managing 17 social media streams.

COST

COST is a simple concept. We all know that increasing value in life requires some form of COST. Groceries cost money. A luxury car costs more money than a standard car. An investment requires a loan. Infrastructure expends labour. Every event has its own budget and its own profit-and-loss statement. COST represents all the financial expenses that any Stakeholder has as a result of the event.

The COST block is an essential part of an event and provides a lot of insight in how the event really works. You do not always have to go into nitty-gritty detail; a general overview can be quite insightful.

When consolidating different Stakeholder perspectives into one Event Canvas, the COSTS of one Stakeholder can be the REVENUES of another Stakeholder. This shows the spider-web complexity of an event as well as the interconnection of Stakeholders. For example, Lee, the artists, and the media people all buy a €25 ticket in the raffle for the photo-editing software. This is a COST for each. For the camera company, sending two reps to the event from the regional office is a COST, as is giving away a product.

QUESTIONS TO ASK

1 What materials and services might be exchanged during the event?
2 What does it take for someone to get here?
3 What does it take for someone to bring their story, goods, message, employees, or service here?

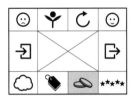

REVENUE

QUESTIONS TO ASK

1   Does this event bring in any money for this Stakeholder?
1   What are the financial revenue streams of the event for the given Stakeholder?

The other side of the profit-and-loss statement from COSTS is REVENUE and is equally an essential part of the budget. REVENUES are financial, or related to financial opportunities, and are related directly to this event.

REVENUE for one Stakeholder can be the COST for another: the €25 raffle ticket COST for attendees is a REVENUE for Lee that helps him offset his COST of the restaurant bill. Some events and some Stakeholders may not have any REVENUE streams.

JOBS TO BE DONE

The JOBS TO BE DONE are the things that the Stakeholders are trying to accomplish in their regular jobs and their everyday lives. They are items on the Stakeholder's to-do list. These can be tasks they are trying to perform and complete, the problems they are trying to solve, or the needs they are trying to satisfy.

Some jobs are crucial to the Stakeholder while others can be trivial. It helps to categorise them by their intent, such as emotional, social, or functional jobs or basic needs. For example, the restaurant has to feed up to 50 people (functional); Lee wants to connect two Stakeholder groups (social); the artists and industry people both have to socialise with strangers, while feeding themselves (social/functional); the camera company representatives want the artists to feel enthusiastic about their new platform (emotional). It's handy to remember that JOBS TO BE DONE usually involve some kind of an actionable verb.

Prioritising the JOBS TO BE DONE from very important to less so provides the design team insight into what tasks need to be handled first.

It's a good idea to get a firm hold of this block early in order to inform how you develop others.

QUESTIONS TO ASK

1 What is this Stakeholder trying to get done?
2 What task are they trying to perform?
3 What problems they are trying to solve?
4 What needs are they trying to satisfy?
5 What is on their to-do list?

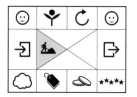

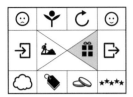

PROMISE 12

1   How does this event create value for this Stakeholder?
2   Why should this Stakeholder contribute?
3   How does the event get his/her jobs done?
4   Does this promise alleviate pains and create gains?

The PROMISE is the 'gift' that attracts Stakeholders to the event, and it presents the basic input for the marketing message. A good PROMISE is concise (in our exercises we ask people to write it as a 140 character tweet), and ideally it can be the same for all Stakeholders. In this way it is to the event what a tagline is for a movie.

A PROMISE describes how the event will relieve PAINS, create GAINS, and accomplish the JOBS TO BE DONE. Lee's PROMISE: 'Picture this: meet + connect with 50 next wave tastemakers over free Saturday lunch.'

DESIGN
COMBINING EXPERIENCE AND LEARNING

The DESIGN group is where the design team will start to talk about the event itself. Until now all the blocks have been part of a thorough Stakeholder analysis and framing the event. This group, and this phase, are the necessary ingredients for the design of the event. These constitute the last two blocks, the top and bottom triangles in the middle: EXPERIENCE JOURNEY and INSTRUCTIONAL DESIGN. They present the opportunity for prototype thinking, to iterate and reiterate within the FRAME to reach the ultimate goal: change of behaviour in the desired direction.

A change in behaviour is realised when people carry what they have learned from an event into their own habitat. To affect this, it's necessary to look at the way people incorporate new information and experiences—how they learn. The four different types of learning:

1 **knowledge-based**
2 **skills-based,**
3 **attitude-adjustment,** and
4 **relationship-based**

These can be split into two challenges: learning by experience and learning by instruction. A person can learn either through instruction or through experience—or, ideally, a combination of the two.
The comparison with raising children is a useful one. You can either instruct them or let them experience the world and learn for themselves. The same is true for Event Design. It is a combination of instruction, as will be considered in the INSTRUCTIONAL DESIGN block, and experience, as in the EXPERIENCE JOURNEY block.

A successful event consists of both an emotional experience and a logical instruction. Planning both during the DESIGN phase gives the Event Design team the opportunity to orchestrate an event flow that will realise the desired behavioural change. You will find that you bounce back and forth between these two blocks, which is all part of creating multiple prototypes.

3 EXPERIENCE JOURNEY

The EXPERIENCE JOURNEY is cumulative moments of interaction that a Stakeholder experiences in the event—listening, reading, watching, debating, mingling, speaking—that build the experience for her. Different Stakeholders have different journeys. The journey goes from the first moment of becoming aware of the event to the last follow up e-mail and every interaction between.

Maya Angelou once said, 'I've learned that people will forget what you said, people will forget what you did, but people will never forget how you made them feel.' This is the experience journey. The results depend on how carefully you sketch the Stakeholders' journey.

Should Lee create a general barbeque menu for people to place personal orders, or create a specific menu of Australian cuisine to make a mark that reminds people of his story, or offer something basic and unfussy so as to not distract from the intended socialising?

QUESTIONS TO ASK

1 What moments of interaction does she experience before, during, and after the event?
2 How does this experience shape the intended behaviour change?
3 Where can you deliver more of an experience than expected?
4 What are the make-or-break moments for any given Stakeholder?

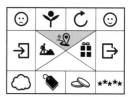

INSTRUCTIONAL DESIGN 14

1 What information does the Stakeholder need to learn?
2 How does he best learn?
3 How can that information best be learned?
4 What skills and knowledge need to be learned?
5 Who does the Stakeholder need to get to know?
6 What attitude needs to be changed?
7 How is that reflected in the schedule and programme?

In close combination with the EXPERIENCE JOURNEY, INSTRUCTIONAL DESIGN is the second half of DESIGN. INSTRUCTIONAL DESIGN covers what needs to be learned and how that is best done.

INSTRUCTIONAL DESIGN is about the content topics to cover, how these are best delivered, by whom, at what time, and at what place. You and your design team will consider which method, format, and interaction is most effective for the Stakeholder to retain the key learnings.

You cannot know anything except that which you have perceived through your senses.

Everything you know is traceable to sensory information. Consider how the INSTRUCTIONAL DESIGN is combined with the EXPERIENCE JOURNEY . It generates the array of interactions a Stakeholder has with the event environment. This is the time to link what you need to learn with how you need to learn it. It is interconnected with the physical environment—down to invitation fonts, carpet textures, cuisine, time of day, keynote speaker versus vendor booth versus pamphlet versus wall plaque, etc. Should Lee give a welcome speech, a closing speech, or none at all? Just a thank-you, or an involved declaration of purpose?

PUTTING IT ALL TOGETHER

CHANGE – FRAME – DESIGN

Fourteen blocks, 3 groups, but what are these boxes for? What is a team supposed to do with them?

The purpose of the boxes and the layout is to guide Event Design teams through their process by generating thought and conversation about all possible aspects of an event, and how to plan for its success. Each box is a conversation starter and a graphic space to organise ideas. Filling out details in a Canvas of your own with drawings, sticky notes, or whatever you choose, working out details for each space, ensures that you will not have overlooked any factor that might affect your event, and that you will take full advantage each Stakeholders' point of view.

The next step is to understand the practical procedures in applying the Event Canvas methodology.

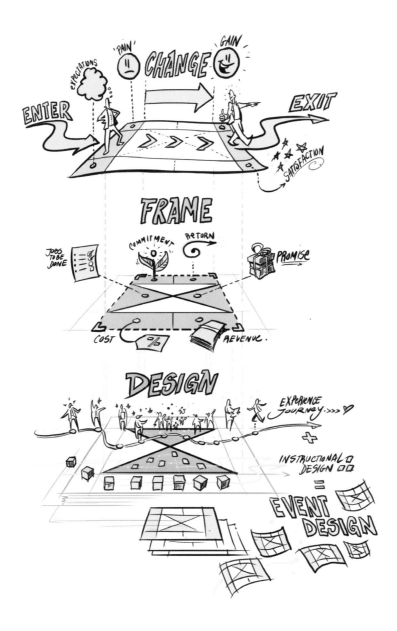

04.

APPLY
EVENT DESIGN

CHAPTER 04

SABINE BONORA

HEAD OF INTERNATIONAL CONFERENCE MANAGEMENT, MED-EL

'The Event Canvas design process allows us to articulate
on one piece of paper the essence of the thinking of
all the stakeholders involved in the event. It creates value,
innovation, and alignment of everyone involved from idea,
to design, to execution, and to evaluation.
After redesigning our pinnacle event, we've adopted it
as the de facto working method for all our events.'

———

Now that you have met the Event Canvas and its constituent blocks, you will presently learn the specific steps to apply it in the process of designing an event.

In order to put this method into practice there are three fundamental resources you will need to secure ahead of time. These are Time, Space, and Team.

TIME

Designing an event in any manner takes time, and designing an event using the Event Canvas is no exception. Spending a preset amount of time on Event Design will save tremendous amounts of time later on in the execution of the event. We recommend as a rule of thumb to claim 1% of the Total Event Time as Event Design Time. We can presume that you want your event to have great effect, and so you will want to dedicate time in order to optimise that effect.

Count on each Stakeholder analysis to take about 60 minutes. We have calculated a time estimator for any given event: design time = (participants x event hours) / 100. This means your team should spend time equal to 1% of the event hours times participants. If the event is 5 hours long and there are 60 participants, design should take 3 hours: design time = (60 x 5 hours) / 100 = 3 hours. The exception is that very large events will need a disproportionately higher time commitment to account for the complexity of large numbers of Stakeholder groups.

SPACE

The process of applying the Event Canvas requires considerable space. You will need to spread multiple canvases in a way visible to a diverse team. You will need a committed room in which to work that offers daylight and provides enough space for a full team to work on multiple posters and flip charts. Ideally, this would be a room in which you can leave these designs in place as works-in-progress and that doesn't have to be utilized for other purposes. Designing is a creative process, and space is a crucial ingredient in that process. A controlled space allows your team to work effectively by revisiting ideas and to be inviting to others to become involved by discovering and contributing to the process.

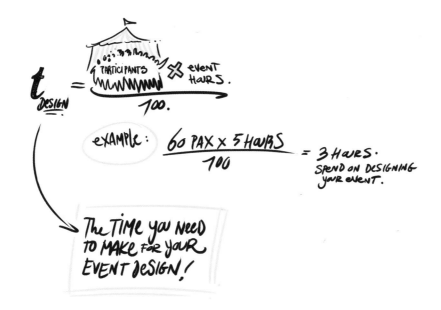

$$t_{\text{DESIGN}} = \frac{\text{PARTICIPANTS} \times \text{EVENT HOURS}}{100}$$

example: $\dfrac{60 \text{ PAX} \times 5 \text{ HOURS}}{100}$ = 3 HOURS. SPEND ON DESIGNING YOUR EVENT.

The TIME you NEED TO MAKE FOR YOUR EVENT DESIGN!

TEAM

Designing is done by a team, preferably a diverse team, with different roles and perspectives, different experience and background, and different preferences. See chapter 7 on the LEAD breakdown. Invite your own team, and invite different Stakeholders (or at least people who have great affinity with various Stakeholders). The more different perspectives you have, the better your design will be. The more diversity in your sessions, the more aligned your team will be in the end.

It will probably take you some energy and persuasion to make these resources available, but it will be worth it.

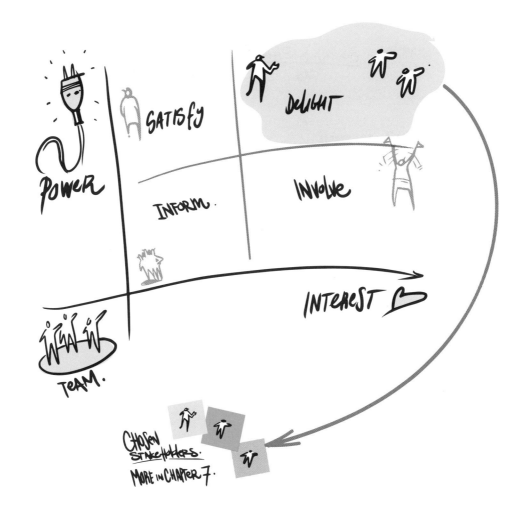

SATISFY

POWER

INFORM

DELIGHT

INVOLVE

INTEREST

TEAM.

CHOSEN STAKEHOLDERS.
MORE IN CHAPTER 7.

THE EVENT DESIGN PROCESS

We talked before about the two basic principles of Event Design:

1 **A successful event changes behaviour**
2 **A successful event is designed for more than one stakeholder**

To start using the Event Canvas, first you will need to identify the Stakeholders involved in your event and make a conscious choice for whom you are going to design the change in behaviour. Once you have made that choice you will articulate their behaviour before and after the event. Based on that analysis and the definition of your Design Frame you can start to make prototypes of an event that will change behaviour.

CHOOSING YOUR STAKEHOLDERS

Your first task as a team is to name everyone who has a stake in the event. Using a flip chart, make a long-list of all the Stakeholders you can think of. This is a brainstorming exercise, so don't discuss; just accumulate all Stakeholders that come to mind.

Next, consolidate, cluster, diversify, and reject any of the Stakeholder groups you brainstormed in the interest of having clear and homogeneous groups.

Then, establish some kind of hierarchy in this list. Ask yourself these questions:

1 **Who could pull the plug on this event?**
2 **Without whom will the event not happen?**
3 **Is this Stakeholder a target group?**

This will help you prioritize how you are willing to dedicate the time you have, and will allow you to design limits on the number of Stakeholders for whom you will be designing.

This is a fairly easy way to identify and select Stakeholders. If your event or organisation is more complex, dealing with much more intricate hierarchies, then you might find yourself frequently referencing Chapter 7, Stakeholder Alignment.

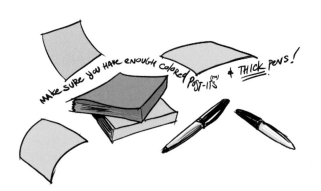

make sure you have enough colored post-its (tm) + THICK PENS!

CREATE ONE LAYOUT PER STAKEHOLDER

Whether you are using the Event Wallpaper or two Empathy Maps and an Event Canvas, you will be working with the same three parts:

1 **Pre-event Empathy Map**
   (Describes behaviour before)
2 **Event Canvas**
   (for the Event Design)
3 **Post-event Empathy Map**
   (Describes behaviour after)

Separately, create an Idea Quarantine: one sheet of flip chart paper that allows your team to park brilliant and not so brilliant ideas not directly related to whatever block or question is at hand. These quarantined ideas come in useful in a later stage, and can even be significant difference-makers.

Have ready sticky notes of different colours, and in large quantities. And have at hand multiple markers ready for each team member. Use one colour for every Stakeholder. You will discover it is very helpful to colour code your work.

Start by filling in the header of the Event Canvas and the Empathy Maps with the (working) title of your event, who you are designing for, the Stakeholder perspective you are designing, your team members' names, the version number, and the date.

SET UP FOR GOING THROUGH THE EVENT CANVAS

Your team should make a Canvas for each Stakeholder that you have defined, in descending order of hierarchy. Either use an Event Wallpaper, or use two Empathy Maps and one Event Canvas. Print either set in large formats (preferably A0 [Dimensions 864 x 1118 mm - 34.0 x 44.0 in - or similar) and hang these on the wall. For a group exercise, working on the wall is much more effective and engages people more than working whilst sitting down at a table.

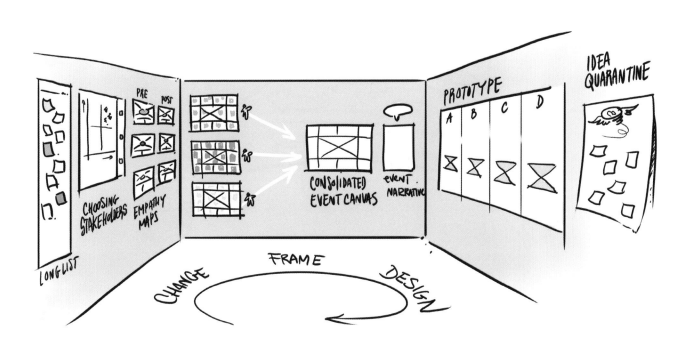

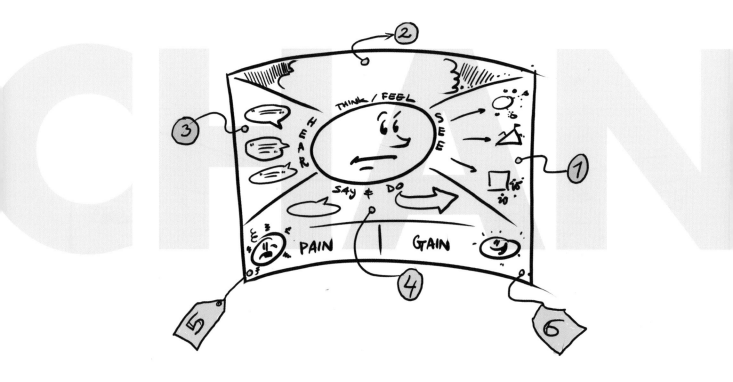

PRE-EVENT EMPATHY MAPS

Understanding different Stakeholders and their perspectives deeply is crucial for designers. You will need to put yourself in the shoes of Stakeholders and identify their key problems and concerns, interests and aspirations, thoughts and feelings, and much more. For some Stakeholders, it might be difficult to describe behaviour—but that is where the Empathy Map proves its depth and power.

The Empathy Map is a map on one piece of paper that consists of 6 blocks, 4 of the blocks aligned around a face. The face is a mental anchor that allows you to easy draw this empathy map yourself. The block in the direction the face looks is called SEE, the block which is above the face corresponds with the brain and is called THINK & FEEL, the block on the side of the ear is called HEAR and the the block at the bottom corresponding with the mouth is called SAY & DO. The two blocks at the bottom are called PAINS and GAINS.

ALIGNING WITH STAKEHOLDERS' PERSPECTIVES

Ask the team to empathize with the Stakeholder by leading them through the following questions. It is important to keep in mind that you are assessing these perspectives independently of the event—what your Stakeholders' experiences are before they ever hear of your event. Use sticky notes in the same colour and have everyone use them to write down their individual ideas of what life is like for the Stakeholder in question. Invite them to put their ideas in the right block. Take 90 seconds per block and follow the following sequence. Do not discuss inputs, it is a lot like brainstorming.

1 **SEE** – What does this person see? What is his environment and what does the market offer?

2 **THINK & FEEL** – What really counts? What are her major preoccupations, worries, and aspirations?

3 **HEAR** – What do friends say? What does the boss say? What do other influencers say?

4 **SAY & DO** – What is his attitude in public? What is his appearance and his behaviour towards others?

5 **PAINS** – What are her fears, frustrations, and obstacles?

6 **GAINS** – What are his wants and needs, his measures of success and obstacles to overcome?

Although all components of the Empathy Map are illuminating, for the purposes of the Event Canvas, it is the SAY & DO section of the Empathy Map that is most critical as it is this understanding that represents the Stakeholder's behaviour before and after the event. To this purpose, start the exercise by picturing a person representing any Stakeholder group as if you were looking at this representative through a camera.

In the next chapter Dave Gray explains why and how he and his team at XPLANE created the Empathy Map.

PANOS TZIVANIDIS

HEAD OF HOSPITALITY, EVENTS & LOGISTICS
INTERNATIONAL OLYMPIC COMMITTEE

'Designing and planning for events is a complicated process by default and requires highly motivated and inspired teams. With the training for designing events by using the Event Canvas methodology, the team was empowered and built the necessary trust in itself to deliver innovative events for all stakeholders of the International Olympic Committee.'

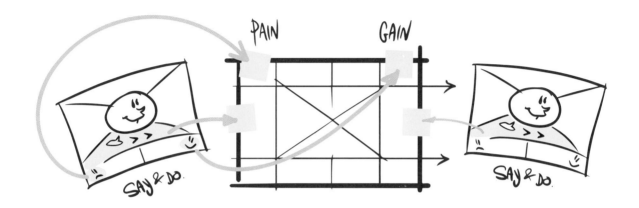

POST-EVENT EMPATHY MAP

Now that you have empathized with this Stakeholder before the event with a Pre-event Empathy Map, you can take a shortcut when it comes to assessing the post-event behaviour. Simply focus on the SAY & DO section with desired outcome behaviours in mind. After the event, what is her attitude in public, her appearance, and her behaviour towards others? Emphasize what this Stakeholder does differently as a result of having taken part in the event.

Now take the sticky notes from the SAY & DO block of the Pre-event Empathy Map and paste them directly into the block ENTERING BEHAVIOUR on the Event Canvas. Similarly, paste the Pre-event Empathy Map PAINS to the Event Canvas PAINS, and likewise GAINS to GAINS. Your last step with the Empathy map is to then take the Post-event Empathy Map SAY & DO and paste them in EXITING BEHAVIOUR of the Event Canvas. You now have 4 of the 14 Event Canvas blocks filled, have put yourself in the frame of mind of your Stakeholder, and have gotten acquainted with Canvas thinking as a process.

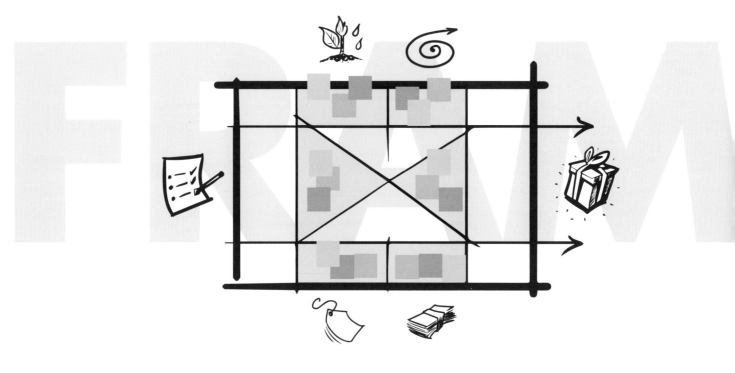

BOUNDARY BOX, JOBS, AND PROMISE

Continue filling out sticky notes for each stakeholder following the Canvas clockwise. Start with COMMITMENT and proceed through RETURN, EXPECTATION, REVENUE, COST, and SATISFACTION, and conclude with JOBS TO BE DONE and PROMISE. Use the QUESTIONS TO BE ASKED sections in Chapter 3 to guide the team through the process.

When you have completed the analysis for all Stakeholders, you can then merge all the Event Canvasses into one master Canvas. This is where you benefit from having used one colour per stakeholder. It might be helpful to see where you can consolidate some different sticky notes (per colour) to keep the Canvas clear and accessible.

ANNALIZA B. LAXAMANA

CEO - LEAD IMPACT ASIA INC

'The Event Canvas gives you a clear perspective of your stakeholders, their objectives for the event, and how you're arriving to meet those objectives. And there's nothing more important than clarity and efficiency when doing an event.'

GERRIT JESSEN
MANAGING DIRECTOR MCI GERMANY

'The process of mapping out
and co-creating events in an
highly interactive environment
is fun, inspiring and result
focused. Simply irresistible!'

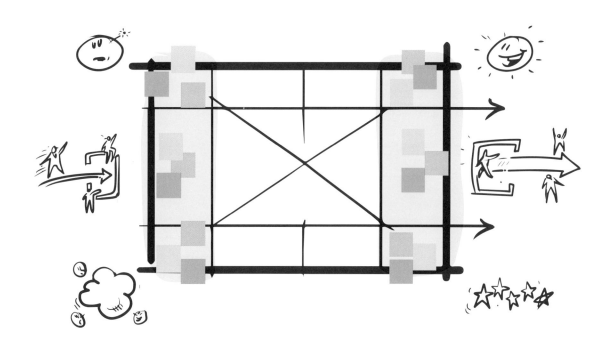

BEHAVIOUR

Now that you have completed a thorough analysis of all Stakeholders and have developed a deep under-standing of each one. You have carefully described for each, their current behaviour (ENTERING BEHAVIOUR) and the desired behaviour (EXITING BEHAVIOUR). Now, look at these behaviours one Stakeholder at a time and articulate the difference in behaviour. This difference in behaviour is what your design needs to create. This is what you will be doing in the next phase.

IDEA QUARANTINE

Based on the articulated behaviour change, verify how the ideas created can teach the skills, knowledge, attitude learning, and/or people learning (who you need to get to know). You can test, iterate, and recombine various combinations of ideas into various prototypes of your event design. Encourage your team to be creative with the building blocks. Suggest the prototype that will work best, within the boundaries of what is possible.

DESIGNING THE EXPERIENCE JOURNEY

Now it's time to do some prototyping and generate some designs. Sketch the journey of a given Stakeholder's moments of interaction that build the experience, chronologically. Start with the invitation and conclude with the follow-up. You have to make sure not only to identify each interaction of the journey, but also how it should create a positive experience.

Remember, Stakeholders will carry with them how you make them feel much more than they will remember any information they have received. Emotions are at the basis of behaviour change.

CREATING THE INSTRUCTIONAL DESIGN

Along with EXPERIENCE JOURNEY the other part of your prototype is the INSTRUCTIONAL JOURNEY. These two play back and forth and allow you to continue cycling through iterations. For the moment, let's consider INSTRUCTIONAL DESIGN. Focus on how your design brings a message across. You have articulated the behaviour change you

aim to see, and based on that change you now identify what the Stakeholder needs to learn.

Break that down into skills learning, knowledge learning, attitude learning, and/or people learning (who you need to get to know). Based on this, create the core elements of the programme of the event. Every element needs to stem from the learning needs of the Stakeholder.

REVISIT THE IDEA QUARANTINE

Is there any odd-ball idea that fits perfectly well with your existing iteration or paradigm? Is there any avenue you forgot to explore.
But don't get sucked in by the charm of the fantastic. It's easy to fall in love with your first prototype. Remember the desired CHANGE, your event's FRAME, and your DESIGN intentions when you revisit the Idea Quarantine. You can always save favourites for later Event Designs if you have something wonderful, but imperfect for the current event.

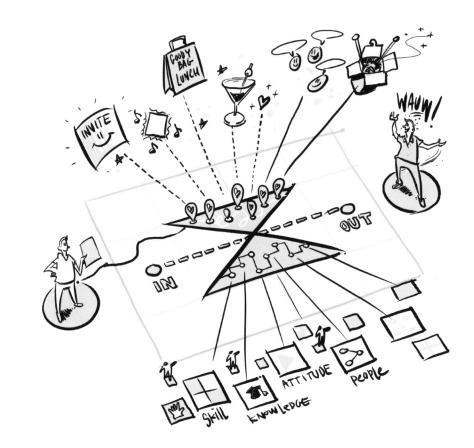

PROTOTYPES

Based on what you have just completed, you now probably have multiple scenarios for the event. These scenarios are rough options of the possible final Event Design. These are your Event Design prototypes. Focus on creating multiple prototypes so your event owner can choose from multiple Event Design alternatives. As a team, determine which prototype is most likely to succeed and propose this back to your Event Owner with pros and cons for each prototype.

CONGRATULATIONS!

Having followed this process, you will have designed an event from multiple Stakeholder's perspectives. Your design should contribute to the change of behaviour of your chosen Stakeholders.

The final step in the Event Canvas process is to solidify the whole object of your designed event. The strategy is to be able to articulate the story of your event concisely, on demand, and use it to 'sell' the design, involve others in the story, use it as a compass for your team, measure outcome, and much more. Remember, you and your team have gone through the process and probably feel quite comfortable at the moment. But others have not had the privilege of hammering out ideas into this productive shape: they have no sense memory of the experience of this process and the energy it took.

So, capture the moment, show the process, and most importantly share the design. You can do this with:

A narrative:
write a story, using the sticky notes as content and the building blocks of the Event Canvas as paragraphs.

A video:
after each phase in the process, and at the end, ask your team to present the Event Canvas and record that on video. This is a very powerful way to engage others and capture all that has been said.

A visual EVENT STORY:
convert your sticky notes into drawings and make the story come to life. Engaging others is much easier if you make your event story visible.

A digital version:
share with others in a digital way, ask others to collaborate and view it online. Find out about the online collaboration tools incorporating the canvasses mentioning in this book by exploring the EVENT DESIGN handbook online resources page.

EXAMPLES

Check out the online resources
and examples at:

 www.eventcanvas.org/resources

05.

MAPPING CHANGE

CHAPTER 05

em·pa·thy
Noun

The ability to understand and share the feelings of another.

People fall in love with products and service experiences as a result of the care that designers have taken to design it with the user in mind.

Bringing the user's perspective and their experience to the forefront is the best way to create what people want. In the previous chapter you have first identified the longlist of stakeholders and then selected those you want to delight. You also came across the need to be empathic with these stakeholders one by one.

If you solve your stakeholder's needs first, they become loyal and you will always win. Conversely, if you are unable to address someone's needs and have not put much thought into designing from their perspective, people have an even finer nose for spotting the missed opportunities in poorly designed services.

Keeping this in mind we want to dig deeper into empathy as a concept. What is the role of empathy, how do you define it, how do you capture such an abstract concept and how do you structure it to extract behaviour before and after an event. And we ask ourselves the question, is it ok to think on someone's behalf?

To do that we are delighted to introduce you to Dave Gray. He is the founder of design firm consultancy XPLANE and he has laid the foundations of the Empathy Map in a canvas. The Empathy map is a canvas we use in Event Design so that teams can empathize with a specific stakeholder and name the "Say & Do" before and after the event.
The "SAY & DO" represents behaviour. The driver of value of events.

Let's meet Dave Gray to share his insights with you on the Empathy Map.

RUUD
Dave, thank you for taking the time to talk to us about Empathy Mapping; it's such a core ingredient in articulating behaviour.

DAVE
It's my pleasure!

RUUD
'What is empathy and why is it so important?'

DAVE
Everyone will have a different definition for Empathy Mapping but my definition is, to imagine as closely as you can or as well as you can what it's like to be that other person. What it's like to walk in their shoes, to experience what they have experienced. I've found that one of the things that's powerful about the empathy map is in a very rapid, very short period of time, someone can go from ... I've seen people go from "oh, I hate this person and I really don't empathize with them at all to actually getting a picture of how they feel." I've seen people really transform their point of view. I don't know that they necessarily are feeling what that person is

feeling, but they're understanding what that person feels.

RUUD
How was the Empathy Map born?

DAVE
We were working with a company, I believe it was Caterpillar, a large industrial equipment company. We were working on an organizational change initiative and we were trying to get a sense of all the people who were involved in the initiative. There were people who were technologists. There were people who were customers. There were people who were engineers and there were a whole bunch of other people.

We were creating a document system that would allow anyone to order parts for their equipment. There were tons of parts on this catalog, and there were a lot of different users, and we wanted to really design this thing with users in mind. There were the people who design the parts. There were the people who upload the parts. There were the people who warehouse and ship the parts. There were the people who need the parts. There were mechanics. There were owners. There were a lot of factors and we needed to really feel like we understood everybody.

We didn't have a lot of time. We drew a bunch of big heads on the wall. That was the first version of the Empathy Map. Before we called it the Empathy Map we called it the Big Head exercise. There are still some people in my company who call it that. We just drew a bunch of big heads on the wall and said, "What are these people doing? What are they hearing? What are they saying? We tried to get a sense of what they did every day. If you notice, the Empathy Map has things like seeing, saying, hearing, doing, and when we do Empathy Mapping exercises, we always start with these things because they are relatively observable.

If you know someone or you have some daily interaction with them, you can imagine what they're saying because you've heard them saying these things. You can talk about what they're doing because you've seen them doing these things. From there, it's not too far of a step to say what they're seeing because you can see what they're paying attention to and often you are seeing the same things. Only after asking those questions do we start asking, what do you think this person might be thinking and feeling? That's the magic of it. It starts with very observable obvious stuff and it moves from outside or external observable evidence and then moves to a leap toward what this person might be thinking and feeling.

A lot of thoughts and feelings are contextual. They are driven not just by who we are internally, but also how our environment shapes and creates us. This makes Empathy Mapping a very powerful exercise. I think that's what makes it work. We start out by thinking that people are the way they are because they're just that kind of person, but when we start to look at the forces that shape that person and start to deconstruct all the environmental factors and the things that are going on, it starts to be a lot more understandable why they might behave the way that they do and why they might say or think or feel the things that they do.

There are not a lot of opportunities, or let's say, in most business situations, we do not tend to focus a lot of effort and attention on understanding what's going on inside of people's heads. Even when you are designing incentives, an area where you would expect we would care a lot about what is going on inside of people's heads, we still treat people in many ways like robots. If we give them more money they're going to do this thing, or if we threaten their job or something, that they will not do this other thing. It's an incredibly simplistic way to look at people. Even in Silicon Valley, which we think of as very progressive, this is still a prevailing attitude.

But people are driven by their thoughts and feelings, and their thoughts and their feelings are driven in large part by the environments they find themselves in.

What we found in doing that exercise was, WOW, this is a really, really fast way to get everyone in the room to a shared and aligned understanding about what actually drives these people, what they care about, what they need, what they want. From there, we went to pains and gains. What are the problems that this person is dealing with? What would our solution get them? What are the problems that they're dealing with right now that cause them problems that our solution is going to help resolve?

RUUD
How have you seen the Empathy Map evolve?

DAVE
Well, a good tool is self-explanatory and very easy to use and I was actually very surprised at how much it took off. It's by far one of the most popular tools that we've ever created at XPLANE. I think that was partly because it's very easy. It's very easy to do. It doesn't try to do everything. It does what it does. It's relatively self-explanatory. It looks really simple, and it is really simple, but it does transform people's thinking. It does help them get aligned about something that otherwise would be very difficult to get aligned about.

I think one of the things that's interesting about it is that sometimes people don't think they need to spend time understanding another person. Usually, when people have something they want to explain, or that they want to do, they have an assumption that they already understand things that they really don't fully understand. They also have the assumption that the people in the room with them have that same shared understanding. Who's our customer? We all know who our customer is. We have it on the wall. Regardless of that, I think even though you may have something written down in a document somewhere, thinking about another person as a real human being and thinking out what's going on inside of them is a very personal matter.

I think part of the reason that the tool like the Empathy Map is effective is that no one can tell you how another person feels. You have to go through that process yourself before you can really have an understanding of what they feel. Going through that process quickly gets people on the same page. They may not always be right, but they're definitely closer than they would have been had they not done it.

RUUD
Why is it so important to go through an Empathy Map as a team?

DAVE
The way that I would explain it is to say, if there are people in the room who haven't been through it, the purpose is not just to do the Empathy Map to understand the stakeholder, it's to get alignment among the team about the stakeholder.

We're not just doing this to create a document. We're doing this to create a shared understanding in the room, in our room, in this room, right now, right here, where we are. If it's something you did but you did it a year ago, well, that person could have changed and also, if we have new people in the room, they may have insights that we have not had in the past.

RUUD
Do you use the Empathy Maps only to extract behaviours upfront or also at other times?

DAVE
We often do the Empathy Map as one of the first exercises on any project, and then we put the map in a place in the room, almost as if that person is there. Then we use it as a stress test for any new idea. It's like, well, okay, we want to do this. Well, let's look back to this person. Look at the Empathy Map Is that going to be exciting to them? Are they going to care about that? We give them a place in the room. They have a spot.

That way they become a participant in the sense that we can go and ask them. A lot of times, what we're focusing on is understanding. If you have some information that you want to convey to them, you want to make sure that you can understand what question they would ask that you're answering. If you can't imagine them asking a question, then they probably don't care about it.

It's like the classic story, where engineers create a product and they love a lot of the features but many of those features are things that customers just don't care about. If you can't imagine them asking a question, then it's a good indication that they wouldn't. If you can't imagine them using a product in this way, then they probably wouldn't. So the Empathy Map also becomes a great filtering mechanism.

RUUD
Empathy Maps represent the stakeholders whilst you design and allows them to ask questions?

DAVE
Indeed, A good example I think in your case would be, what questions would they ask about this event? What am I going to learn? Who's going to be there that I know? Who's going to be there that I want to hear from? At the beginning you want to create an event that's interesting to this person. What questions can you imagine them asking you about this event? Do I have to go? Why should I go? Why would this be better than me staying at work and dealing with my emails?

RUUD
Is there a risk of group think or any pitfalls that you see in using empathy mapping in specific environments? Group think meaning that people are just going to give the desired answers and will not be giving their true answers.

DAVE
I think even if they give their true answers, there's always danger of groupthink. The danger of groupthink in some ways can be increased when you use a tool like this, because you are forcing the thinking in specific directions.

'So if empathy is the core element of good design, the ability to empathize with a specific stakeholder is at the core of good Event Design.'

One thing that this is very useful in helping to mitigate the groupthink is the diversity of people that you bring into the room in the first place.

If everyone already knows each other and they already worked together and they already spent a lot of time together, that creates a danger of groupthink right there. Sometimes as a facilitator, because you don't know them, you can be a guide there but sometimes it might be helpful to increase the number of people in the room to try increase the diversity of ideas.

The second thing that I've noticed that increases the danger of groupthink is: If you just have people talk instead of doing sticky notes.

When you ask people to answer a question and they put their answers on sticky notes quietly first, and then share, you get a much greater diversity of ideas than if you just give them the Empathy Map and ask them to talk about it.

Let's say you say, "Okay, what is this person saying?" You start at one person and you just go around the table, and each person says. Whatever the first person says will anchor the whole conversation and then everyone else, yes, oh yes then something similar and yes, just like what he said or what she said.

But if you have them write on sticky notes, and you have them think quietly to themselves before they share, that helps.

THE PROCESS OF EMPATHIZING

As a former CEO of IBM stated, very insightfully, "Good design is good business." The reason why it matters for organisations is because Design Thinking is the single biggest competitive advantage you can have. So if empathy is the core element of good design, the ability to empathize with a specific stakeholder is at the core of good Event Design.

In Chapter 2 we discussed two sides of a relationship in user-centric design that work in conjunction: behaviour change and empathy. Both topics are difficult for a team to manage because they seem to fall into the emotional realm, and they are remote. How do you specify the emotional, especially when the subject is not immediately available? Rest assured, these processes do not have to be purely emotional exercises. They can be precise, analytical, inductive, and deductive.

In this chapter you have examined the preferred tool to quantify empathy.

In the Empathy Map, you and your team now have the tool for making the process of empathizing quantifiable and the goal of influencing predictable. You don't have to be afraid to think on someone else's behalf. Doing this as a team will align your thinking. Having identified the behaviour change whilst empathising is a powerful exercise, critical to the success of Event Design. And later, in Chapter 7, we will explore a tool to tame the prospect of influencing change of different stakeholders.

ABOUT ME

Dave Gray is a leader and manager with a background in design. He is the founder of XPLANE, a strategic design consultancy firm, and co-founder of Boardthing, a collaboration platform for distributed teams. Dave is the author of two books: Gamestorming and The Connected Company. His area of focus is the human side of change and innovation, specifically: How can you get people to adopt new ideas?

EVENT DESIGN CASES

ELSA'S
8TH
BIRTHDAY

PERMA
FORUM

SOL

NAE

INTERCOMMUNITY
(INTERNET SOCIETY)

SES

The best way to internalise what you have just learned is to apply it yourself. Bring yourself back to the last event you witnessed, you organised, you visited, or that you were responsible for. Documenting existing events is a smaller step than to start designing a new event. In this way the Event Canvas is the only new factor and you just need to apply the thinking to something you have seen in action. Designing from scratch brings at least two new factors to the table; the Event Canvas and a blank sheet of paper to begin with. So start documenting an event you know well to get familiar with the Event Canvas first. You might want to see some examples, to better understand applied use of the Event Canvas and to appreciate existing designs. Existing designs can be a possible resource and may trigger your thinking and encourage you to start designing.

ELSA'S 8th

BIRTHDAY PARTY

PRIVATE EVENT

CASE 01

ABOUT ELSA

How would we explain the use of the Event Canvas to our very own kids? We decided to use an event we can most probably all remember, our 8th birthday. A real-life case study told from 3 perspectives: Elsa who is turning 8, her parents, and her grandparents. Elsa's birthday is the perfect moment of celebration for the whole family and an opportunity for everyone to get together.

EVENT CONTEXT

In a few weeks time Elsa will celebrate her 8th birthday. Grandpa and Grandma really want to spoil Elsa. Mom and Dad want to make it a memorable day for everyone! Elsa really only wants one thing: a brand new iPad mini.

WHO IS ORGANISING THE CHANGE?

Elsa's parents are organising Elsa's 8th birthday and putting everything in place to make it a picture-perfect family moment involving Elsa as the most important Stakeholder.

WHAT WAS THE CHALLENGE?

Think back to your very own 8th birthday party. The most important thing to the birthday girl or boy is getting presents, which remain a secret until the big day. The challenge at hand is to satisfy that most important thing for 8-year-old Elsa, but also getting the family together around her birthday and making sure everyone's needs are met.

WHO ARE THE MAIN STAKEHOLDERS?

Elsa's father and mother are the event owners. They decide who is invited, when the party is being held, and how the party will take place. The guest of honour is Elsa, who is a key Stakeholder in this birthday party. Last, the grandparents are key Stakeholders who wish to be part of this important celebration for their grandchild. All want it to be a family moment to cherish.

THE EVENT DELTA

Before the event Elsa is 7 years old. The day of her birthday, turning 8, is symbolic for Elsa. For the parents, Elsa's birthday is the perfect moment of celebration for the whole family and an opportunity for everyone to get together. 'What should we get her?' asks Mom as she is already planning this family moment in her mind. All Dad can think about is how much Elsa must love her dear parents, and making it the party a picture-perfect occasion.

'The best moment is realizing that the party was a success for everyone.'

—— Just by looking at all the stakeholders

EVENT NARRATIVE

For as long as she knows, Elsa is looking to get connected with her friends and be able to play with them as much as possible.

She knows it's her birthday in a couple of weeks and she is dreaming up what she will be getting as a gift.

So what is truly on the mind of an almost 8-year-old?

You guessed it; her very own iPad mini.

'Hard to imagine that Elsa was born nearly 8 years ago?' says Dad. 'It seems like yesterday we were holding her as a baby in our arms.'

'Do you really think we should get Elsa that iPad mini?' Grandma asks as she thinks of her sweet granddaughter Elsa. 'Yes, of course. Let's spoil her now that we still can,' responds Grandpa.

Both Grandpa and Grandma can't wait to get iPad lessons from Elsa and spend precious moments online using FaceTime to connect with her between birthdays and other family events.

And so it went. Mom baked a beautiful birthday cake, Grandpa and Grandma were delighted to offer Elsa her very own iPad mini, and Dad realized his perfect moment with photographs to treasure.

Elsa turned 8, got her very own iPad mini, and everybody lived happily ever after.

THE DESIGN PROCESS

Of course, you would think organising a kid's birthday party is something parents have been doing across the world without the use of an Event Canvas. But in their minds, the exact process that is used to design complex multi Stakeholder events is happening in the most natural way.

There is an entry behaviour and an exit behaviour. There are certain functional, social, and emotional jobs to be done as well as basic needs. There are pains and gains for Elsa, the parents and the grandparents. They commit the time to plan the day, bake the cake, buy the gifts, and take the pictures. The return is the time spent together as a family and family love that is visible to all during this special day. The expectations are Elsa receiving an iPad; the promise is the smile on Elsa's face, the pleasure for the grandparents of connecting with their granddaughter, and the picture of the family moment for posterity. This all comes at a cost, and ultimately the behaviour change where Elsa's exit behaviour of no longer being 7 but now turned into an 8-year-old daughter and granddaughter connected to her friends and family through her brand new iPad.

THE BRAIDING POINT

When does each Stakeholder start to think about this birthday party? And when they do, what are the next steps they take to get the birthday party planned. These braiding points could be at different times for Elsa, who already looks forward to her 8th birthday months in advance; the parents, who start planning for the invitations to go out probably weeks in advance; and the grandparents, who commit to going to the birthday party and buying a present for Elsa.

Everyone's experience journey and instructional design is different. The grandparents may want to ask the parents what Elsa would really like for her birthday and be informed about what the parents are getting her so as not to duplicate the same gifts. The parents need to keep the gifts secret, telling Elsa only that she will get a gift. The amount, level and timing of the anticipation of having the family all together on this special day makes for different braiding points when each Stakeholder becomes involved in the event.

NEXT?

It's a Giant Leap from a birthday party to a high-stakes event. But in essence, it comes down to a multi-Stakeholder approach and a change of behaviour. Any event, even something as natural as a birthday party, can be understood better by dissecting it with the Event Canvas. A birthday party might not seem as a high stakes event in comparison to a corporate event, but the stakes are high to the Stakeholders involved, and so the conscientious design, of the event makes the difference between success and failure, even if the owners can't put a name to the steps they've taken to ensure success. What if Elsa ever attains a position where she could use the power of events, knowing the lessons of her birthday party and the use of the Event Canvas?

ELSA

THE BIRTHDAY GIRL TURNING 8

'WOW, now I understand why my birthday is so important to YOU and Grampy!'

FERMA FORUM

FEDERATION OF EUROPEAN RISK

MANAGEMENT ASSOCIATIONS

CASE 02

ABOUT FERMA

In today's competitive business environment, Risk Management—defined as 'managing the threats and opportunities to our businesses within acceptable risk tolerances'—plays a vital role in the success of all businesses.

Risk managers bring their professional expertise to this discipline and to corporate governance. Increasingly throughout Europe, organisations employ risk managers, whose function embraces risk identification and mapping, risk control, and risk financing, including insurance.

In many countries across Europe and beyond, National Risk Management Associations are well established. Their members are risk and insurance professionals responsible for risk management in their organisation, whether in the public or private sector. FERMA provides the means of coordinating risk management and optimising the effect of these Associations within the European continent

EVENT CONTEXT

Every two years, FERMA holds its well-established Risk Management Forum, always located in a different country with the support of the local member association. It also organises specific seminars and surveys.

WHO IS ORGANISING THE CHANGE?

The group needing to design behaviour change is the FERMA Forum committee consisting of volunteer leaders of the federation together with a local organising committee of the hosting country that reports to the Board of Directors of FERMA.

WHAT WAS THE CHALLENGE?

The bi-annual Risk Management Forum is a major European conference designed by risk managers to give all risk managers the opportunity to meet their European counterparts and international and local consultants or service providers. It allows them to exchange knowledge on how they can help and influence business decisions to ensure good management standards, and how to integrate them into the business processes of their organisations.

WHO ARE THE MAIN STAKEHOLDERS?

The FERMA Forum is designed for two key Stakeholders: 1. risk managers, and 2. insurers and brokers. Both are members of a National Association of Risk Management, which is in turn a member of the Federation of European Risk Management Associations.

THE EVENT DELTA

Living and working in a riskier world. Risk managers are the core Stakeholders who are on the demand side of identifying and mitigating risk for their organisations. They enter the event with a need to connect to other risk managers who are in the same role in other organisations. Together they learn about the latest developments in the field. They exit the event inspired to address challenging situations because of the enhanced network of contacts from the Forum. They are more confident having been educated about the latest risk patterns and trends, and are ready to influence others in their organisations about risk management. The insurers and brokers exit the event with a new set of enhanced relationships. They have been able to connect on a social level away from the negotiations table and are primed with opportunities to provide insurance and coverage for risk with their new and enhanced risk manager contacts.

EVENT NARRATIVE

The risk manager lives and works in a risky world, always on the edge. He is balancing each risk and seeks backup for those risks. His jobs to be done are to educate himself and to network and share with peers, brokers, and insurers. He leaves the FERMA Forum connected to a community of other like-minded risk managers well balance with new knowledge, fresh insight, and new and broader networks so that his risk are managed in a much more balanced way.

His pains are being alone in a corporate environment working on risk. His gains are discovering that others have a similar role in other companies doing exactly the same thing and the possibility of reaching out to them and getting in touch with insurers and brokers to mitigate risks.

His expectations are that the FERMA Forum is a quintessential event in the field.

Satisfaction is to have had a great experience—time well spent in a friendly environment with all the key players in the market represented. The cost is the registration fee; there is no direct revenue.

The commitment is 4 days out of office and a weekend away from family. The return is to have an up-to-date and broader understanding of risk management and of the consistently changing dynamic environment.

The insurer is there to cover the risk manager's risks she wants to mitigate, to carefully tailor a product around each case. Her jobs to be done are to interact with the risk manager, manage accounts, calculate risks, and offer solutions. She leaves the FERMA Forum with new prospects and ideas on how to follow up with existing clients.

The insurer's pains are to meet as many prospect risk managers as possible. At the FERMA forum, the insurer can have a pied-à-terre to interact with the Risk managers in a friendly environment. His expectation is to be able to meet the risk managers in a friendly environment. The insurer is represented by his CEO in the insurer CEO debate, and high level contacts are established with key clients in the one-on-one meetings in private meeting rooms onsite or in VIP lounges/buses. This is the place to meet the top people in the risk management arena, and time is well spent away from the claims and pitch environments outside of the Forum. The insurers are significant contributors to the FERMA Forum financially and have extensive evening social functions to entertain their key audiences. Their commitment is 4 days out of the office and preparation time to get the appointments lined up. The return is a very efficient set of high-level meetings all in one place during the 4 days—a place for friendly encounters and renewed strategic business relationships.

THE DESIGN PROCESS

FERMA Forum takes place once every two years and is a significant contributor to the bottom line of the organisation. It's success has a big impact on the federation. In this edition, the organisation chose to analyse the 2013 edition carefully in order to better understand where the success of the event comes from in order to identify critical key design components.

THE BRAIDING POINT

The event was audited by 3 event design specialists from 2 different generations who each individually mapped out their participation in the Ferma Forum on an event canvas. They visited the even anonymously and documented the experience journey and the instructional design using photography, video, analysis of social media and interviews onsite. The views were consolidated and reported back with specific recommendations to the FERMA board for subsequent editions.

NEXT?

The event was documented in an Event Canvas and used to brief subsequent editions of the event on the mechanics and critical success factors of this edition of the event.

PIERRE SONIGO

SECRETARY GENERAL, FERMA (FEDERATION OF EUROPEAN RISK MANAGEMENT ASSOCIATIONS)

'The Event Canvas will relieve pains in organizing our congress because it gives us a process and a common language for understanding. Everyone involved can then go in the same direction with the canvas as the roadmap to keep us on track. I really believe this is going to help us a lot!'

SOL
INDEPENDENCE DAY
HEINEKEN

ABOUT SOL

Sol is a Mexican beer that originated in 1899. The company believes in Espiritu Libre and celebrates those who live with a Free Spirit. After centuries of thick colonial beer, a maverick German brew master wanted to give the people of Mexico a light, refreshing beer. And so he created El Sol, which would later become Sol.

EVENT CONTEXT

In 2014, the Global Marketing Manager had a daunting sales target. He felt he had only one chance to rally his sales and marketing forces after his predecessor tried numerous times to push the brand and failed.

WHO IS ORGANISING THE CHANGE?

Heineken is one of the leading brewing companies in the world. It is a global multinational company with operations in 70 countries and reaching 178 markets, each served by National Marketing Managers. The Global Marketing Director for Heineken had in Sol an orphan brand that had been available for 10 years, but was only selling in 5 markets. Sol's main competitor had and continues to have global recognition, and it dominates the class to which it belongs. The Sol brand had lost its credibility in markets at the local level across the globe. Marketing it was an uphill battle and marketing managers preferred to spend their resources on more recognizable and successful brands.

WHAT WAS THE CHALLENGE?

Marketers argued that making it a success would take too much time and would take too long; they didn't have any budget to give the brand the necessary support.

WHO ARE THE MAIN STAKEHOLDERS?

There were two Stakeholders: 110 international senior marketers and CMOs on one hand, and the Global Marketing Manager of Craft Beer and Sol Cerveza on the other hand.

THE EVENT DELTA

The desired change was in the attitude of 110 international senior marketers and CMOs toward the brand. Sol needed to change their attitude of not believing this brand could make them more successful into one of believing. But attitude was not the only thing; the 110 marketers were expected to act and feel responsible for the brand. The event was intended to give them conviction.

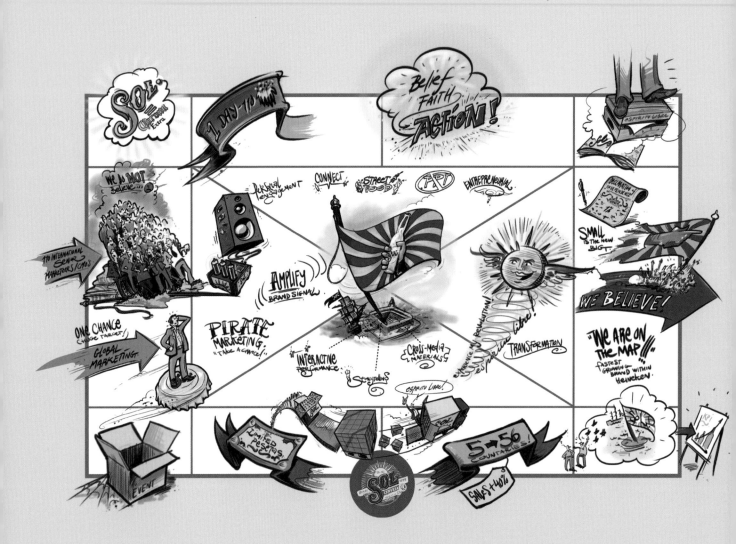

EVENT NARRATIVE

The desired exiting behaviour for the marketers was that they would believe in the brand. A key aspect of the Sol Independence Day was, to demonstrate their belief, the marketers needed to sign a Declaration of Independence and join the 1% of the Heineken community who believed in Sol. The Global Marketing Manager felt this was a critical step in putting his brand on the map and for it to become the fastest growing brand within Heineken.

Both Stakeholders' JOBS were to amplify the brand in their region. Reverting back to the roots of Sol was reverting back to the soul of the brand: the Mexican Revolution and Espiritu Libre, the free spirit. That Espiritu Libre was the PROMISE for the marketers and CMOs. Normally in big corporations, everything needs to be played by the rules. But Sol is an exception, and this took the form of Espiritu Libre.

As a joint PAIN, both Stakeholders felt that the brand Sol was not distinctive enough and was always referred to as 'something like Corona'. The GAIN was that the brand book of Sol allowed everyone to tell his or her own story about the brand', encouraging the marketers to take personal responsibility for it.

Everyone expected an 'inside-the-box' event in which the speakers would use Powerpoint and again direct the marketers to sell more of this particular brand. Instead, every marketer present was sharing the story about Revolution and how they were part of the transformation.

Sales went up 45% and the number of countries where Sol was served went from 5 to 56.

SO HOW DID THEY DO THAT?

The event happened on a fortress just in from the shore, and the EXPERIENCE JOURNEY consisted of a mixture of personal engagement, entrepreneurial spirit, human connection to the brand, and the feeling of a street food festival.

The INSTRUCTIONAL DESIGN consisted of interactive performances, storytelling, and cross-media materials. And there were no Powerpoint slides.

THE DESIGN PROCESS

Event marketing agency MOVE took the challenge and designed the Sol Independence Day for Heineken. The stakes were high because there was only one chance for the brand to reach its Stakeholders. It was very likely that repeating what had been done in earlier events would result in the same stagnation as before. Focussing instead on behaviour change helped to direct the event design conversation to a more innovative and effective design. MOVE challenged their client to think differently and came up with a groundbreaking design to achieve the desired behaviour change.

THE BRAIDING POINT

The Global Marketing Director, responsible for this orphan brand 'Sol', did not know what to do because nobody believed in the brand and he had an enormous sales target. His predecessors tried to promote the brand internally, numerous times without success.

NEXT?

MOVE uses the Event Canvas to start conversations with their clients, such as Heineken, and many others, to involve them in the Event Design. The Event Canvas enables MOVE to facilitate the discussion around the design and align their team and the client's team.

VERA KURPERSHOEK

SENIOR PROJECT MANAGER, MOVE

'The Event Canvas allows us to bridge the gap between consultancy and practical event organisation to create insights on all stakeholders' interests. A perfect tool to craft and deliver events worth attending.'

INTERCOMMUNITY

INTERNET SOCIETY

ABOUT THE INTERNET SOCIETY

Founded 23 years ago by Vint Cerf and Bob Kahn—two 'fathers of the Internet'—the society began as a not-for-profit organisation to support Internet standards development. It continues in that role today as the administrative home for the Internet Engineering Task Force, and is also involved in a range of activities related to Internet technology, public policy, and access and development. With headquarters offices in Reston, Virginia, and Geneva, Switzerland, the Internet Society now has an international membership of more than 140 organisations, 78,000 individual members, and 111 chapters worldwide.

How do you bring together people from around the world who are the heart and soul of the Internet?

EVENT CONTEXT

The Internet Society, born in 1992 to look after the Internet, meets in many places across the globe but never simultaneously on the Internet, even though the Internet is their subject. In 2015, it was time to open up the Board of Trustees meeting to all the members of the Internet Society by coming together in a completely new way.

WHO IS ORGANISING THE CHANGE?

When Kathy Brown joined the organisation as its new President and CEO, she knew that in order to advance their mission, 'The Internet is for Everyone', it was imperative for this society to create its very own innovative event. Together with her leadership team, she launched the idea of an event about the Internet on the Internet just a couple of months after joining the organisation.

WHAT WAS THE CHALLENGE?

How do you bring together people from around the world who are the heart and soul of the Internet and who are dedicated to its open development and its universal accessibility? The Internet Society answered that question with InterCommunity 2015, the organisations' first global meeting of members, held 'on the Internet for the Internet'.

WHO ARE THE MAIN STAKEHOLDERS?

This event will enable the Society's 70,000+ global members, 111chapters, 140 Organisational members, and experts across the Internet technical community (IETF) to come together using the Internet through a network of interconnected events across the world. This meeting sets a new precedent and showcases how the Internet can facilitate engagement and connections across distance and time.

THE EVENT DELTA

Before the event, the three core communities
(Members, Organisational members, and the Internet
technical community) had only limited interconnecti-
vity and awareness of each other's activities. The Board
of Trustees consists of representatives of each of these
communities. After the event participants will have
seen the Board of Trustees interact and open communication among the three communities in a way that
had not been seen before.

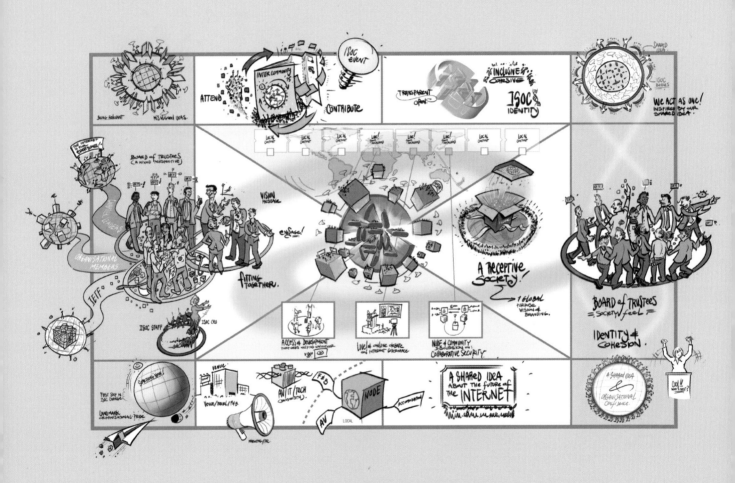

EVENT DESIGN CASES

EVENT NARRATIVE

The Internet Society takes on many of the most important and challenging issues facing the Internet—and it does so on a global level.

The Internet Society Board of Trustees, at its 119th meeting, decided to hold the first-ever virtual Global Community Forum for the Internet Society's world wide membership to be called 'InterCommunity 2015'. Held in conjunction with the Board's Annual General Meeting in Auckland, New Zealand, the event 'followed the sun', featuring concurrent, real-time forums around the world connected through the Internet to create one, hybrid global meeting. It ran from 20:00 UTC on 7 July 2015 to 09:00 UTC on 8 July 2015.

InterCommunity 2015 was designed to showcase the power of the Internet to transcend boundaries and to unify the Internet Society around the globe through an exchange of knowledge and ideas. This meeting enabled the Society's 70,000+ global members, 111 Chapters, 140 Organisation members and experts across the Internet technical community to come together virtually through a network of interconnected events across the world.

The InterCommunity 2015 was hosted from SkyCity in Auckland, co-located with the InternetNZ NetHui conference. Forums were set up across Asia, Africa, Latin America, North America, and Europe that were interconnected as part of this global meeting. The Internet Society Board of Trustees, President and CEO Kathy Brown, and limited support staff were present in Auckland, while the Executive team and staff were positioned at regional events closest to their base cities.

Fifteen regional node events were hosted across multiple time zones. Internet Society Members could access preliminary event details on the InterCommunity page in Connect, and non-members were encouraged to join the Internet Society to take part.

Enabling the communities of the Internet Society to connect using live meetings and the Internet during this first InterCommunity event allowed the Internet Society Board of Trustees, at its Annual General Meeting, to engage and involve Chapters, Members, and other community partners.

This first step in creating a new global hybrid event was a first for the Internet Society and allowed the core communities to discuss and debate essential topics. These included Access and Development, live online debates on Internet Governance, as well as node and community discussions on Collaborative Security.

By attending and contributing, participants took part in a global conversation looking to reinforce the shared idea about the future of the Internet.

Discussions highlighted diverse perspectives and were transparent, open, and inclusive to create a cohesive and receptive society with a clear purpose, vision, and brand. It is not just the best idea, but the shared idea that will create organisational confidence, identity, and cohesion in this first step in Internet Society change. InterCommunity 2015 became an organisational landmark using the Internet to connect the Internet Society.

THE DESIGN PROCESS

Over a span of 6 months, by using the Event Canvas methodology, a wide cross-section of staff was involved in the creation of this brand-new global event. The event took place across the globe on 7 and 8 July, 2015, starting in Auckland, NZ and following the sunrise across the world to connect the Internet Society across all time zones in 24 hours.

Using the Event Canvas framework, we synthesised inputs from dozens of people and from there were able to identify to six core Stakeholder groups, mapping out needs, goals, and metrics for each of them. One result was the emergence of three key areas of discussion for the meeting: Internet governance, improving security and trust on the Internet, and ensuring Internet access for everyone in the world.

Given the ambitious scope, technical logistics, relatively short, six-month planning window, and other factors, projections for the first-of-its-kind event were modest, but in the end it far exceeded expectations. Stakeholders, even those on the technical side, were surprised and flabbergasted to experience what an Internet event could be. InterCommunity 2015 set a new benchmark in this space.

InterCommunity allowed individual viewers who were not physically present at one of the 15 regional nodes to engage through a chat tool within the event's interface, and to participate in polling and surveys using a social quesrion-and-answer app as well as social media. Attendees at regional nodes could interact with each other and, in most cases, with other nodes, as well as with the Auckland host site. The Internet Society used small touches and details to build community identity, from kicking off the program by showing individuals from around the world holding identical photo frames branded with the InterCommunity logo, to ending each of the two global sessions by having participants at the host and remote locations simultaneously launch paper airplanes.

THE BRAIDING POINT

The ability to 'do work' as an organisation and to challenge to take on one central new task was at the core why it was important to create this event. The challenge gave the full organisation a reason and a litmus test to work cohesively.

Right after launching this big idea live at a regional Chapter Leader Workshop in Budapest, President and CEO Kathy Brown was made aware of the Event Design methodology using the visual Event Canvas to align Stakeholders and design an event from scratch by a team. Seeing an example of the Nuclear Security

Summit on an Event Canvas caught her attention to encourage the team to adopt and try this new Event Design methodology.

Within weeks, the Internet Society staff team applied the Event Design Methodology. They diligently long-listed the Stakeholders, focusing the conversation on alignment of the needs and defining their measures of success of those that need to be delighted. Multiple teams worked side-by-side in a set of 6-hour design sprints to empathise with the key 6 Stakeholders. These laid the foundation to frame the design of the event on the event canvas.

Ideas generated by the teams who joined the event design sessions from Washington, DC, Geneva, Amsterdam and Montevideo were aggregated using online collaboration tools and ranked for feasibility and importance.

Prototypes of the event were created and presented back to the decision makers to select the one that would work best for this first edition. The event narrative was created and then sketched into the Event Canvas to tell the story of the event. The Event Canvas formed a compass for the team to now get approval, market the event, and execute it with a common understanding of this first InterCommunity event.

It goes without saying that many were nervous, after months of planning, debating, creating content, testing, and worrying about the event. Though it was venturing into the unknown, the event was well prepared and when the event was 'on' you could feel the excitement and engagement in 'realtime'.

The sense of achievement, pride, and energy of delivering on it collectively, collaboratively, and successfully was a key performance indicator for the organisation and the community as a whole. InterCommunity was a landmark event for the Internet and set a new benchmark in the space.

NEXT?

With this first milestone set, the organisation is now gearing up for the sequel to this inaugural InterCommunity. In hindsight, the first edition was a proof-of-concept that such connected events truly are possible, and it will be used as a steppingstone to prepare for the 25th Anniversary of the Internet Society, which is currently being designed by the staff team using the Event Canvas methodology, just like they did for the first edition.

NAE DAY

DUTCH ACADEMY OF

EATING DISORDERS

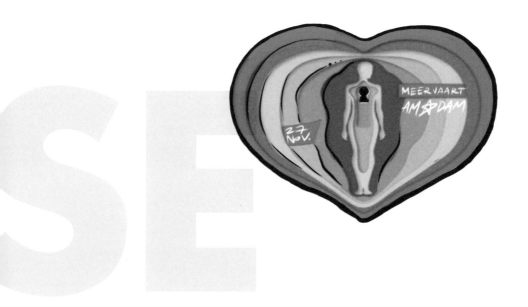

ABOUT THE NAE

The "Nederlands Academie voor Eetstoornissen" (NAE), or the Academy, is committed to leadership in eating disorders research, education, treatment, and prevention. Members can be individual practitioners as well as institutions focussed on patient care in the field of treating eating disorders. The pillars that the Academy has built itself upon are sharing knowledge, educating, networking, fostering cooperation through multiple disciplines, and acting as advocates.

EVENT CONTEXT

NAE has a biannual meeting cycle. In the even years NAE organises the NAE Congress, and in the odd years NAE licenses an event called NAE Day to one of its member organisations. The NAE Day 2015 was licensed to Human Concern. The reason for licensing is to offer a sneak peek into a member organisation's practice.

WHO IS ORGANISING THE CHANGE?

Human Concern is a member organisation of the NAE. Their concept, vision, and approach are different from those of other treatment practices. Human Concern works with experience professionals. These are professionals who, in addition to their professional designation and accreditation, have overcome an eating disorder themselves. These professionals use this experience actively and purposefully in their client treatment, which is perceived as unprofessional by most of their peers. Human Concern hired ByBabs—an event agency based in Amsterdam managed by Babs Nijdam to help them design the event. Babs introduced the Event Canvas to them after she had followed a workshop about the Event Canvas methodology. She helped her client's core team to frame the discussion, analyse stakeholder perspectives, and design the event using the Event Canvas as a template.

WHAT WAS THE CHALLENGE?

Making every Stakeholder comfortable with the direction in which this event was going was the main challenge for the designers. They had to acknowledge and respect different Stakeholders' perspectives. The Event Design was the result of Empathizing with every Stakeholder carefully and every one of them could recognized their own perspective.

WHO ARE THE MAIN STAKEHOLDERS?

For this event, three Stakeholders were identified: NAE, represented by the board; Professionals in the field of Eating Disorders; and Human Concern, as the licensee of the NAE day 2015.

THE EVENT DELTA

The designed Event Delta is to scale concerns in the eating disorder field back to the individual human experience, to see the client as a human being, and to find the balance of cure and care in treatment. Allowing professionals to use their own experiences is a taboo and that is exactly what makes Human Concern successful. The goal was to shift this paradigm by bringing back the human scale and proving its value.

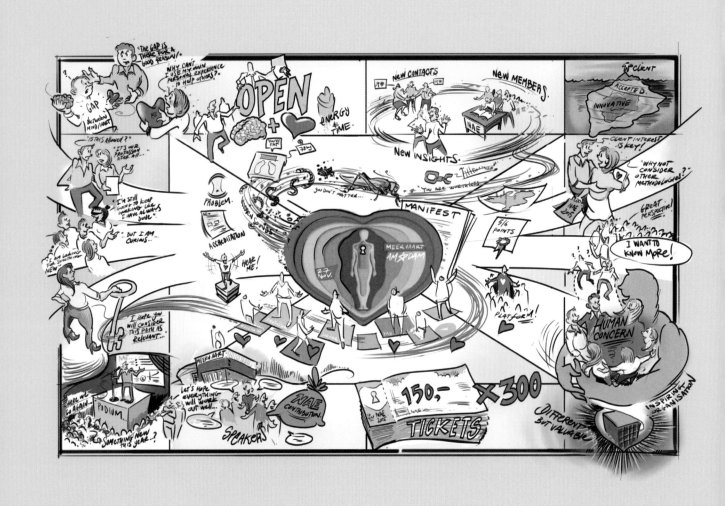

EVENT NARRATIVE

ENTERING BEHAVIOUR

The NAE is safeguarding the treatment of clients and is concerned with whether the approach of Human Concern is allowable. The professionals in the field are looking to learn and get new insights on the treatment. Human Concern is proud and confident about their approach and sees this opportunity to showcase and prove their successful treatment.

PAINS

The main pain is the gap between heart and mind, which is where Human Concern places its emphasis. The NAE claims that this gap exists for a reason. Professionals, of whom significant numbers are in this field because they have overcome their own eating disorders, question the reasoning behind the strict separation between heart and mind: why wouldn't you share some of your own experiences?

COMMITMENT

The commitment of all Stakeholders should be; come with an open heart and an open mind, and, of course, invest time and energy in this event.

RETURN

The intended outcomes for every Stakeholder, when they travel home, are that they each develop new contacts, new insights, and for NAE specifically recruiting new members.

GAINS

Reach the mutual understanding that is important to put the client first, create clarity in the industry about what is accepted, what is innovative, and how to position different treatments. Establishing a conversation which is not about right or wrong but about different approaches.

EXITING BEHAVIOUR

As desired exiting behaviour for the NAE, the team focussed on guiding them to developing an open mind: why not consider other methodologies, and far more importantly, putting the client first. The professionals are intended to have a new and fresh perspective on the use of their own experiences as professionals in treatment. And Human Concern gets recognition and is seen as an inspiring organization.

EXPECTATION

All Stakeholders have a certain expectation of the event, based on previous experiences and the fact that Human Concern is the organiser this year. They expect presentations from the stage supported with Powerpoint, and they feel that this year the event could be something new and different.

SATISFACTION

All Stakeholders should feel, when leaving the event, that it was valuable and different, something where the passion for curing and caring for others were the primary consideration.

COSTS

Venue, logistics, and speakers, as well as a contribution (as a licence fee) to the NAE, are the main cost elements.

REVENUE

The budget was based on having 300 professionals signing up for an average fee of 150 EUR.

JOBS TO BE DONE

As an overarching job, the team identified a common interest and common care for solving the problems associated with eating disorders. NAE's event cycle tells them to organise an annual event. The professionals need to continuously educate themselves, they need accreditation points, and they need to maintain and develop a network. Human Concern is looking for the platform to share their passion and their care for their patients.

PROMISE

The main reason for participating is different for each Stakeholder in this case. NAE's promise is to organise events, provide education and accomplish geographical spread of their events involving member organizations. For the professionals the promise is that they will be introduced to a way to get accreditation points, to talk to peers, and to immerse themselves for a day in learning about new treatments and insights. For Human Concern the promise is a that they will have a platform upon which to be clear about their approach, and to share their passion.

THE EVENT DESIGN EXPERIENCE JOURNEY

To enforce the message of putting the clients first, Human Concern designed a special experience designed to put all participants in the shoes of a client, to show and have them experience how clients feel. Participants are measured in different ways; they have to stand on a scale and the result is put on a sticky note. That note is fixed to the person's back so everyone, except the person wearing it, can see it. There is a constant audio feed during the breaks that whispers thoughts clients have, such as 'You are too fat', and, 'You don't matter'. Also during the breaks participants are offered insects, considered by some as high protein nutrition and by others as something too grotesque to eat. These exercises reflect the world of people with eating disorders. Furthermore, the decoration is similar to Human Concern's interior decoration, to stress the human aspect rather than the clinical aspect.

INSTRUCTIONAL DESIGN

The instructional design is a mix of experience sharing of (former) clients, best practices, and presentations by international speakers. Eighty percent of the speakers are professionals who have overcome an eating disorder. Formats are tailored to the message and there is a focus on dialogue, conversation, and storytelling. The Human Scale is the theme of the NAE day, which is a combination of bringing issues back to human proportions, seeing the client as a human being, and treatment as a balance of cure and care. In addition, there is art by former clients displayed in the venue and there is a lunch with former clients.

THE DESIGN PROCESS

To organize an event as a licensee is special for many reasons. First of all, organising events is not the organization's core competency. And second, at that moment, there was no alignment between the licensor and the licensee and no common language to have a fruitful conversation. Last but not least, all the Stakeholders had considerably high stakes in this event. The licensee needed a common language and process to use to be respectful to each of the Stakeholders' needs.

THE BRAIDING POINT

Babs Nijdam was hired as a consultant to help Human Concern design and organize this event. Babs was heavily inspired by the simplicity of the Event Canvas as a design tool and needed a process not just to help her client execute this event, but more importantly that she could use to design events. The analysis of all stakes and event story resonated really well with Human Concern's Managing Board.

NEXT?

As a result of having seen this process form the sideline, its output, and the meaningful conversations this process led to, the NAE decided to use the Event Canvas as a design tool for their future events.

BABS NIJDAM

OWNER, BY BABS

'Consulting my client using
the Event Canvas process
helped me align the stakes and
design with the end in mind.'

07.

INFLUENCING FOR SUCCES

In chapter 4 you discovered how you can use the Event Canvas methodology to design your events and create a story. Every event story has characters; it might be two, or it might be many more who are involved in the event.

Your Event Design team who creates the event story also has different types of characters. In order to get your story together, the characters on your team have to explore the strengths and weaknesses they each have.

There are 3 important moments when you design:
1 **Choice of Stakeholders;**
2 **The right team**—if you don't have the right team your design process will not get to where you want to go;
3 **Getting the event owner's approval by influencing the decision of the final decision maker**—understanding the preference of the decision maker and using their language to get buy-in for the proposed prototype.

In this first part of chapter 7 we will cover how to choose the right Stakeholders using the Stakeholder alignment process. In the second part this chapter we will cover how to assemble the right team, as well as how to understand your decision makers based on their preferences and how to influence them effectively.

COMPLEX STAKEHOLDER ENVIRONMENTS

Sometimes things are not as simple as they seem—as you've seen in the cases, you and your team have to be aware that your event may have a different complexity. There may be more than two Stakeholders whom you need to align.

For example you may have seen the Internet Society's InterCommunity Case study. Up to 16 Stakeholders were considered at first, and then the number eventually narrowed down to the 6 core Stakeholder groups.

Or consider the dynamic you may experience when you are designing a global sporting event in which internal and external Stakeholders need to become aligned in order to have a consistent experience. Imagine dealing with an executive board, a local organising committee, sports federations, sponsors, athletes, and live and online viewers. Every stake has a different view, different preference, different interest, and unequal power over the decisions being made.

In some cases, you may even discover that a Stakeholder you considered to be part of the event should not have been so considered in the first place, or should no longer be part of it after the event evolves over time.

But if you have such a large number of Stakeholders, how do you get to the right Stakeholders? How do you choose them and how do you align them?

When you have a complicated story with multiple Stakeholders and many storylines, what you need to do is align the stakes of each of these Stakeholders. You need to be clear as to which one of the Stakeholders you are currently designing for. Who do you need to delight, who can you just inform and who needs to be involved with you?

Making these choices is something you can do with your Event Design team using a process called the Stakeholder Alignment methodology. Subsequently, you will be exploring how your team functions, using the LEAD method. LEAD is also a terrific way to figure out how to best influence the decision of your event owner, depending on her specific personal preferences as an individual.

Meet our trusted friend Dave Bancroft-Turner, Managing Partner of MatrixTC, a company that has developed, tested, and refined these methods across the globe successfully.

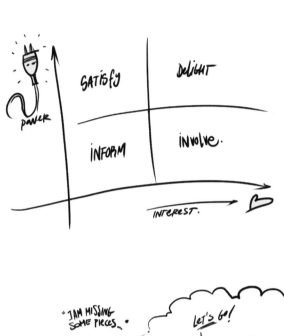

STAKEHOLDER ALIGNMENT

L.E.A.D.

DAVID BANCROFT-TURNER
MANAGING PARTNER, MATRIXTC

THE STAKEHOLDER ALIGNMENT TOOL

Getting your Stakeholders aligned with what you are doing can be a mighty difficult task. Some Stakeholders appear from nowhere and can stop you immediately and some Stakeholders can make life very difficult for you if they feel that they have not been involved or informed as to what you are doing.

So we are going to introduce you to two tools that will make your life a lot easier and will make the Event Canvas work even more effectively.

We will cover an influence and communication tool to guarantee success—it's called LEAD—after we cover the Stakeholder Alignment tool.

In organisational life we get many messages from management.

These are common ones and should be familiar to you.

You need to:
- get closer to your Stakeholders
- find out the agenda of your Stakeholders
- ensure you know what they want
- find out their needs
- find out what their critical measures are.

All of this is very sensible, but sometimes very difficult to achieve, particularly if the Stakeholders aren't in the same country, let alone the same office.

A frustration heard from people when they are asked to focus on the needs of their Stakeholders is that they say, 'What about my needs? What about what I want? Why is it I have to focus on their needs? I have needs as well, you know, and nobody seems interested in them!'

'A Stakeholder is somebody who has an interest in your success.'

—— So yes, it's a person, not a thing

There's good news: If you follow a core process,
1   You will find out what really is important for your Stakeholders
2   You will find out what isn't
3   You will have a tool to reduce conflict in your Stakeholder relationships and between Stakeholders
4   You will do less work and have more time
5   You will develop a closer working relationship that will have all sorts of benefits
6   You will finally get your needs on their agenda.

The process is called Stakeholder Alignment.

It has six stages and they are procedural, that is, you follow one after the other. Some of you will like that; but for those of you who don't, just follow it—the process doesn't work if you skip steps.

First, do you know what a Stakeholder is?
It's a bit of organisational jargon isn't it?

Well it is dead easy. Here is the definition: a Stakeholder is somebody who has an interest in your success. (So yes, it's a person, not a thing.)

All you will need is a piece of A4 paper, some sticky notes, and a pen. Oh, and a business problem, a challenge, or a new task, job, or role—anything job-related so you can have a go at using it for real. For the purposes of learning the process we are going to use a generic example to bring it to life. Once you understand the process then you can apply it to any work-related issue.

To make this easy for you and your team, we've created the Stakeholder Alignment Canvas download at www.eventcanvas.org/resources

'Our AIM is to get to the top of Mount Everest and return safely.'

—— So, let's get started

STAGE ONE

Decide on your aim. An aim can be anything—as small a task as needing to design a new logo for a client, or as big as starting a new job. To use our example task, if we are going to climb Mount Everest the aim could be defined as something like, 'To get to the top, and back down again, safely'.

Notice there is no minutia, no timescales, no money or budget, no detail of any type. That's because it's an aim. An aim is a general direction of where we need to go. It is a direction-finding statement.

STAGE TWO

Having decided your aim, it's time to think about those 'tricky' Stakeholders that you have in your world (all those lovely people that you have to work with). Stakeholders can be many different people. If you look at your aim, you may come up with a long list. Put one Stakeholder at a time on a sticky note and add them to the Stakeholder long-list. (I'll tell you why in a minute.)

You've got Stakeholders like:
- The team that is going up the mountain
- Our friends
- Our families
- The boss (and perhaps even the boss's boss)
- Mountain rescue
- Our doctors
- The Government of Nepal (we do need a visa)
- Our insurance company
- Other climbers
- The Sherpas
- Local hotels
- Local shops
- The weather people (or 'Meteorologists' which is very difficult word to fit onto a sticky note!)
- Travel agents
- Airlines
- Fitness instructors (we all need to be fit!)
- The media
- Equipment suppliers

(Let's stop there for the sake of not using up more paper and ink.)

This list of Stakeholders will always depend on your aim. If that changes, so will your list of Stakeholders. Once you have these labels on your sticky notes you are now ready for Stage Three.

STAGE THREE

Looking at the people on your sticky notes, you have probably noticed that some are more important than others, right? Good, because now we need to do some prioritising. On your paper (a flip chart is good, too) you need to draw two intersecting lines and put these four words in each of the quadrants. In the top right corner add the word 'Delight'; Top left hand corner, the word 'Satisfy'; Bottom left quadrant write 'Inform' and the bottom right hand side, 'Involve'.

You have a matrix with two axes: Power (Low at the bottom to High Power at the top) and Interest (Low Interest to the left and High Interest on the right).

'**Delight**' is the quadrant for Stakeholders who have the power to stop you immediately and have a high level of interest in what you are doing, and are therefore the most important group. (In the Everest example the Sherpas that we employ to help us get to the top would be a good example, as would our partners in the team.)

'**Satisfy**' comprises Stakeholders who also have some power, but have a lower level of interest in you. However, if they are not satisfied, they can make life difficult for you. It's a bit like going to bed with a mosquito: very annoying, but not life-threatening. In the Everest example, the Local Government office that issues the climbing licences is in this category.

'**Involve**' covers who you need to involve because of their special interest.

'**Inform**' covers who you need to inform during the process.

If we represent '**Power**' and '**Interest**', the Stakeholders look like this

IMPORTANT!

Now, discuss with your climbing colleagues each Stakeholder in turn and place the relevant sticky notes in one of the four quadrants. It is important that you agree, so some discussion will be necessary. For most aims there is normally an even distribution between all quadrants, but don't worry if that is not the case.

This phase is critical because we need to be clear within the Team about the relative importance of our Stakeholders. If there is any misalignment between us when we are on the mountain, our behaviour can be deflected in different directions, which may prove lethal! In the workplace, people don't normally face true life-and-death decisions, but the usual outcome is conflict, ambiguity, arguments, etc.

STAGE FOUR

The Stakeholders that have ended up in the **'Delight'** quadrant are the ones we will specifically be designing this event for. We now need to do some work by thinking about their needs and how they will measure whether their needs have been met. So, the best way to do this is to prepare one piece of paper per Stakeholder, draw two columns, and label them:

- **Needs**
- **Measures**

If we take a Stakeholder such as 'Our families' in the climbing of Mount Everest, a completed example may look like this:

If we were to continue, we may end up with eight or nine different needs for each Stakeholder. The secret is to keep it to a manageable amount—always on only one side of A4 paper. Do the same for all Stakeholders in the **'Delight'** quadrant. It is sometimes easier to do this if you involve trusted colleagues in the process.

STAGE FIVE

The secret to getting Stakeholder Alignment is to take the document to the Stakeholder in person (or virtually if they are elsewhere) and check for accuracy and feedback. They may well have a different view of some Needs and Measures, and that is okay. Doing so may help reduce your workload and also provide true clarity over what is important for them. This Stakeholder validation is a powerful way to have a very valuable conversation.

STAGE SIX

Now you have a window of opportunity to show your Stakeholder another paper: the one you have previously prepared with your needs on it. This is the only way we know of, for getting your agenda on the agenda of some challenging Stakeholders. Take this opportunity to be very clear about what you need. It may be your only chance!

With the process mentioned above, you have now identified and selected the Stakeholders to design for (the ones in the Delight quadrant) and identified their 'JOBS TO BE DONE'. You can use these directly in the Event Canvas.

TRUST THE TEAM + TRUST THE PROCESS

Just a good team or just a good process won't deliver good design; the two have to work hand-in-hand.

Now let's take a closer look at the individual preferences people on your team may have and why it is important to understand their behavioural preferences. Learn about the dos and don'ts in you approach to each of them individually and about their role in your Event Design team. Ultimately, when you believe in the diversity of your team and trust the process of Event Design, you will achieve results you hadn't thought imaginable.

LEAD – The Communication and Influence tool to make your life a lot easier

Turning now to the LEAD Communication and Influence tool mentioned above, we are going to explore the different communication preferences that people have and introduce you to a model that, when used skilfully, will provide you the tools you need to influence almost anybody.

People are different, right? Their differences mainly arise from varied preferences for doing things and varied ways of interacting with the world and others. These preferences are mostly unspoken and covert. The model covers:

- Why people may prefer to do things differently
- What these unspoken preferences are
- What the four major personality preference types are that exist throughout the world
- How to identify these four different preferences
- How to change your communication style to influence others even better

We have preferences for lots of things: the cars we drive, the friends we have, the holidays we go on, the ways our houses are decorated, the food that we eat. Preferences are reflected by:

- The way we interact with others
- The way we make decisions
- The way we take in information
- The way we process this information
- The way we communicate

What's amazing about human beings is that all of us (from a DNA perspective) are very similar, with the only major differences linked to these unspoken preferences. The key question is what these differences are and how they affect someone's ability to influence others, particularly when that someone has little or no authority.

Before we proceed, a warning: the following exercise employs some stereotyping, and we know that people are more complicated than just four categories allows. However, the model called LEAD does so in order to provide a conscious process and set of tools that we can all use to systematically influence others without them knowing (including your wives, or husbands, and children).

LEAD-ing the way

This graph shows two different axes that chart the four major categories that help us answer the question, 'Why do people do the things that they do?' On the y-axis, North relates to how 'Thoughtful' people are. These types of people, when faced with a problem, would prefer to think about it, sometimes for a long period, before discussing with others.

South on the y-axis is the opposite, where the 'Talk-Full' person has a preference for talking about the same problem before thinking or processing the issue. Have you ever been faced with a 'Talk-Full' person recounting an issue in his life when you have been thinking to yourself 'Why are they telling me this?' They are telling you because it helps them process and answer their problem. They put their developing thoughts into the world to see what they get back. The process involves talking first, which helps 'Talk-Full' people think. The opposite is true of the people who fall along the North axis. They rely on thinking first before talking. Imagine a partnership or marriage where each person is an extreme example of both, will this be heaven or hell?

On the x-axis, West is related to what we call 'Concealing'. People have different levels of comfort (or preference) for what they reveal of themselves. The 'Thoughtful' person typically conceals personal information because, to them, the world is about data, process, logic, and quality. The 'Talk-Full' person typically focuses on the task at hand, getting the job done, speed, and activity.

East on the x-axis is 'Revealing'. The 'Thoughtful' person will typically express their concerns, their troubles, their needs, and their fears. Whereas 'Talk-Full' person will typically divulge information as to what could be or might be—the future and their view of the possibilities.

Plotting on these two axes reveals four very different types of individuals—we call them Logical, Empathy, Action, and Difference, or what we refer to as the LEAD model. All are valid and are what we call a 'preference'.

Thoughtful

Methodical	*Overly Formal*	**Considerate**	*Self-deprecating*
Systematic	*Risk-Averse*	**Supportive**	*Stubborn*
Organised	*Inflexible*	**Friendly**	*Gossipy*
Efficient	*Aloof*	**Caring**	*Naive*
Careful	*Cold*	**Kind**	*Sulky*
Factual	*Sceptical*	**Trusting**	*Gullible*
Objective	*Obsessive*	**Practical**	*Dithering*
Structured	*Patronising*	**Sensitive**	*Smothering*
Conscientious	*Bureaucratic*	**Agreeable**	*Overly-emotional*

LOGICAL   EMPATHY

ACTION   DIFFERENCE

Direct	*Loud*	**Visionary**	*Temperamental*
Decisive	*Selfish*	**Expressive**	*Indecisive*
Sociable	*Bullying*	**Creative**	*Disorganised*
Confident	*Arrogant*	**Easy-going**	*Unfocused*
Pragmatic	*Dogmatic*	**Inquisitive**	*Unpredictable*
Resourceful	*Aggressive*	**Flexible**	*Subversive*
Competitive	*Antagonistic*	**Innovative**	*Absent-minded*
Determined	*Domineering*	**Playful**	*Daydreaming*
Extraverted	*Confrontational*	**Open**	*Argumentative*

Revealing

Conceiling

Talk-full

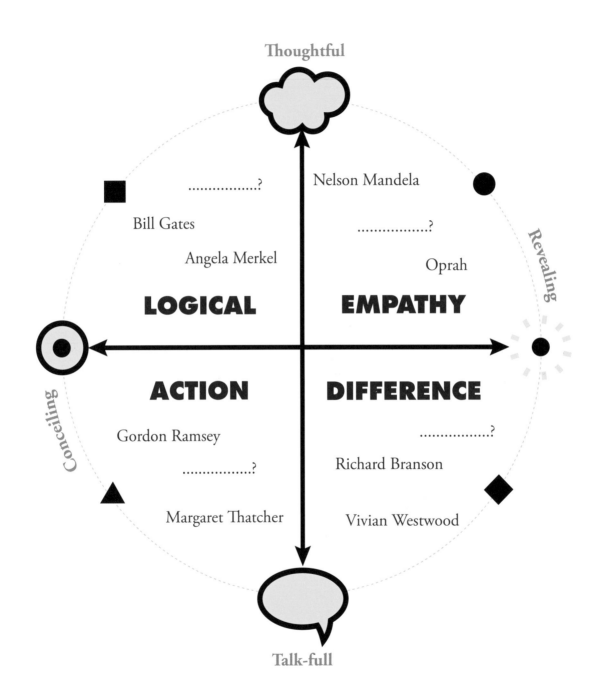

Thoughtful

Nelson Mandela

.................? ●

Bill Gates

.................?

Angela Merkel

Oprah

LOGICAL **EMPATHY**

Revealing

Conceiling

ACTION **DIFFERENCE**

Gordon Ramsey

.................?

.................?

Richard Branson

Margaret Thatcher

Vivian Westwood

Talk-full

People can, of course, have any preference at different times, but a good comparison is to think of 4 different radios all playing different types of music: rock, jazz, classical, and country. For most people, one of these radio stations is turned up quite loud, which means it drowns out the other three. It is also likely that one of the radio stations will be very low. This will therefore not be a preference. A 'preference' means that when you are in a comfortable place in your life, when times are good, then you will naturally fall into one of these quadrants.

We all face a difficulty when we seek to influence others who have a different preference. Have a look at the typical positive attributes (those listed on the left under each of the four preferences on the graph on the previous page). You may recognise yourself in one of the quadrants from this list, or perhaps two quadrants equally represent you. When these behaviours are overly present or presented in the wrong situation, they then become weaknesses (those listed on the right in italics under each of the four preferences).

Looking at the typical behaviours for each of the quadrants, it is easy to see that the way in which each type prefers to be influenced is very different.
- **The Logical preference** needs information, uses logic, and demands accuracy and quality.
- **The Empathy preference** needs to be inclusive, uses relationships, and demands involvement and consideration.
- **The Action preference** only needs summary information, uses speed, and demands activity and clarity.
- **The Difference preference** needs options, uses creativity, and demands excitement and difference.

Thinking of real or fictional people can not only provide some light relief, but can also offer a good handle to the stereotypes. For example
- **Logical:** Bill Gates, Angela Merkel?
- **Empathy:** Nelson Mandela, Oprah Winfrey?
- **Action:** Margaret Thatcher, Gordon Ramsay?
- **Difference:** Richard Branson, Vivian Westwood?

THE LOGICAL PREFERENCE

People with LOGICAL as a primary LEAD preference will typically demonstrate behavioural restraint; self-control and self-discipline; will prefer planned and organised actions, rather than spontaneous or unexpected events in their lives; are methodical and systematic in their work; take themselves seriously and favour projecting a formal, professional image to others; and prefer workplaces that give them routine, order, stability, and structure.

They can occasionally be quick to judge the behaviour of others and often find it difficult to appreciate opinions or practices that contradict their own orderly approach towards thinking, working, and being. They can also sometimes act dismissively towards people who subjectively generalise, are reckless, or seem overly emotional. Their preference for analysis, rigour, and planning highlights their need for people to maintain a calm professional detachment when influencing them, and for others to provide them with clear communication and structured solutions.

THE ACTION PREFERENCE

People with ACTION as a primary LEAD preference are excitable, talkative, gregarious, positive, and extraverted; often have a large circle of acquaintances; and tend to adopt a task-focused approach towards work and problem solving. They can be quite socially confident, charming, persuasive, and pragmatic; and typically prefer working in predictable structure or environments that give them a sense of place, position, purpose, or power.

Their need for recognition and praise, social interaction and excitement coupled with their enthusiastic and often no-nonsense approach towards clearing obstacles to achieve their goals can often be misinterpreted as arrogance, 'showing off', bullying, or aggression. When being influenced, they desire an emphasis on the speed, simplicity, and results that will be delivered because, to them, 'actions' speak louder than words! They prefer positive communication that are focussed on tasks or outcomes, and simple solutions that are free from ambiguity.

THE DIFFERENCE PREFERENCE

People with DIFFERENCE as a primary LEAD preference are imaginative and interested in new, novel, or unusual ideas and future possibilities. Their often disorganised, unhurried approach towards work can be confusing, annoying, funny, or distracting to people, especially if they 'bounce' from one random idea to the next, or when they antagonistically challenge restrictive practices or people with inflexible views or controlling behaviours.

They usually have lots of creative ideas and like to spend time thinking or talking about starting lots of various projects. Because they are easily distracted, they can frequently abandon a plan for one that seems to be more interesting or different. When being influenced, they want people to be as tolerant of ambiguity, relaxed, intellectually creative, curious, challenging, liberal, and open-minded as they are, and prefer people to talk about potential and future options, rather than restrictive or rigid single-approach solutions or ideas.

THE EMPATHY PREFERENCE

People with EMPATHY as a primary LEAD preference will typically work hard to create and maintain harmonious relationships using considerate, caring, and kind behaviours; are usually genuinely concerned for the welfare and wellbeing of others; tend to have an optimistic and trusting view towards people in general; and prefer workplaces that are collegial, friendly, inclusive, co-operative, and sensitive towards the needs of others.

They prefer environments where respect, trust and shared values exist and can become upset, withdrawn or stubborn if their offers of help are rejected, their sensitivities are ridiculed, or their trust is broken. They'll avoid confrontation because of its potential for damaging relationships and will often ignore the unacceptable behaviour of others in order to maintain peace and harmony. When being influenced they prefer people to be sensitive to the needs of others; and provide inclusive solutions that seek to reduce animosity or uncertainty.

Let's get back to the practical application of this model. Each of the four preferences needs to be influenced in different. Read each one in turn and mark next to the page the name of your team member that you can apply to each preference.

The skills that relate to this part are as follows:
- You need to understand your own preference(s) and how they drive your own behaviour
- You need to appreciate that not all people are built the same way as you
- You need to be able to spot the preference(s) of your Stakeholders so that you can...
- Be flexible in your own behaviour to meet the needs of others; it is then easier to influence them.

You will need to practice how to spot the 4 preferences. You may find it is relatively easy to categorise many people based on your previous experience with how they behave.

The various dos and don'ts require practice, but will have a major effect on your ability to influence others in your world. The good news is that you have the rest of your life to practice!

Here is the 'gold dust' for you; we have already done some of the work for you. We have introduced the four LEAD preferences and a range of what you need to do and not do when you meet with these types. To examine the dos and don'ts for influencing each of the four preferences or to find out more about the diagnostics; check the cards in the online resources here: www.eventcanvas.org/resources

SOURCE

The LEAD model was presented by Dave Bancroft-Turner in this chapter. It has been created by Dr Wayne Thomas of MatricTC. For further information, review the additional resources on www.eventcanvas.org/resources.

If you would like to find out more or confirm your own or other's preferences, then you can complete the LEAD model diagnostic 84-item questionnaire. The results will be sent in the form of a booklet that provides comprehensive information on how to influence the four preference types in even more detail.

ABOUT ME

David Bancroft-Turner has been a trainer, coach and facilitator for the past 20 years after a successful career in Financial Services. He specialises in Leadership Development and continues with his pioneering work in the area of Organisational politics and Matrix Management. He has worked with many organisations in the Event Industry and has been a top speaker for many years.

His book 'The workplace politics pocketbook' was published in June 2009 and has been reprinted twice.

DAVID KLIMAN

OWNER, THE KLIMAN GROUP

'Highly usable strategic roadmap, easily customized, and very suitable for use by professionals seeking to enhance their strategic impact on meeting content and flow. I was very curious to learn more about this and was very impressed with all aspects of the Event Design Certificate workshop. I highly recommend it!'

CECILIA LJUNGLÖF

CONFERENCE MANAGER, KTH ROYAL INSTITUTE OF TECHNOLOGY

'It's an inspiring process for everyone involved in designing the event. The Event Canvas makes it easier to work with my stakeholders to design their event without getting locked into pre-existing thinking patterns.'

08.

BALLS, BARRIERS & BALLOONS

'There are three responses to a piece of design - yes, no and WOW! Wow is the one to aim for.'

MILTON GLASER

GRAPHIC DESIGNER

Having developed and applied the Event Design methodology as described in this book across the globe with a team of very diverse (organisational) cultures, geographies, and languages, we would like to share with you some insider tips that will make you a game-changer and give you the edge. Along the way, we have made more than our fair share of mistakes and have tried and tested many different ways to design events. Allow us to share some of our biggest common mistakes and insider tips.

Great Event Design doesn't (always) guarantee a great event. However good your event design, it remains an exercise on paper that then needs to be realized by a team who know how to deliver events.

Rest assured; the design you have created on the Event Canvas is the best briefing document any event planner could wish for. Knowing the Stakeholders you need to delight, their ENTRY and desired EXIT BEHAVIOURS, what each Stakeholder EXPECTS, their PAINS, JOBS TO BE DONE, and at what COST and REVENUE levels you are going to deliver the PROMISE, as well as having a clear picture on the COMMITMENT of resources of time and expected RETURNS, will prime the execution of the event.

BALLS & BARRIERS

COMMON MISTAKES AND HOW TO AVOID THEM

If you can't do it on paper, you can't do it online. Start your team off using good old paper versions of the canvasses. It's tempting to use glitzy technology options to get your team started on event design, but trust us, if you can't do it on paper, you can't do it online. That doesn't mean we are against online tools, to the contrary, we have some excellent tools where our templates are available to enable remote teams to collaborate on their designs using easy to use drag-and-drop tools maximizing time and defying distance.

 TIP: Collaborate online with your team using preset templates.

MIXING STAKEHOLDER PERSPECTIVES

Make sure you don't sow confusion when it comes to which Stakeholder you are designing for. A common mistake is to complicate things when mixing up Stakeholder views. Writing the Stakeholder name in each of the headers and repeating it prior to doing video recaps is no luxury. It will kindly thank you if you are disciplined doing this whether this is your first Event Design cycle or if you are a veteran. Using colour codes per Stakeholder with a clear legend right from the start is the best insurance against this classic mistake.

TRYING TO PLEASE EVERYONE

You can't please everyone, so get over it. Select the Stakeholders you need to delight and focus just on them. Limiting your design to only this select group takes a little getting used to at first, but you will see that it works.

TIP: Use the Stakeholder Alignment Canvas (and check Chapter 7) to find out who needs to be delighted.

BEING CONFUSED ABOUT TIME

Be mindful of the way perceptions of time can vary. To the left of the Event Canvas is before the event, to the right is 'after' the event. All sticky notes you add to the canvas need to respect what the Stakeholder does or should do as a result of having attended the event. Time can be both your enemy and your friend; use it to your advantage to make the most of the team's creativity, energy, and dynamics.

TIP: Use the Timekeeper role and the time indication on the facilitation cards as a best practice guide.

MIXING

Mixing Event Design and Event Planning in the JOBS TO BE DONE section of the Event Canvas. The Event Canvas is not intended to be a checklist for all the JOBS TO BE DONE by the event planner, so don't fall into the trap of listing items like: Send out 'save the date', open registration system, send out mailing etc. The JOBS TO BE DONE by the Stakeholder are independent of whether there is an event or not. The JOBS TO BE DONE need to be done, either through participation in the event or in some other way.

PUTTING TOO MANY IDEAS ON ONE CANVAS

Describing too many different ideas in the same Event Canvas can lead to confusion. Try using separate Event Canvases to sketch each prototype of your event design. You can always combine ideas at a later stage.

PROTOTYPES ARE NEVER WRONG

No prototype is wrong. It could be that it just is the wrong time for the prototype your team has produced.

EVENTS ARE NOT ALWAYS THE SOLUTION TO THE PROBLEM

Have you considered if you would not do the event at all? Should it be a movie, a campaign, or promotion instead? If you didn't launch an event, what would be left unaccomplished, what behaviour would not be changed? Not doing the event is your easiest and cheapest prototype and one you must always consider in motivating your design prototypes.

TRYING TO MAKE THE BEST EVENT CANVAS EVER

You and your team get overly excited when designing the event and trying to make the best Event Canvas ever. Remember it is not about making the best Event Canvas, it's about making the best Event Design.

VISUALS AND WORDS

As you discuss ideas in your team, and write them onto sticky notes, beware not to be too wordy (or verbose is better). You're looking for quick visual references and visual impact. Including visual elements in your design sketches can be powerful as reminders to yourselves and as talking points when introducing ideas to event owners—after all, visuals are processed much more quickly than are words alone.

Try to be as succinct as possible in writing your notes, and find opportunities to couple imagery with your words. But even if you leave out images, if you don't have a sketch artist in your group or you don't generate pure visuals, consider that the use and layout of sticky notes on the canvas is itself a graphic representation of ideas on its own.'

GRANULARITY AND LEVEL OF DETAIL

When you're designing, think big picture: take a step back and choose the right level of granularity for the Stakeholder you're dealing with. Getting into minute details will distract you and delay your Event Design unnecessarily.

GETTING STUCK AFTER THE EVENT DESIGN FRAME HAS BEEN SET

Once you have the design restrictions in place, you might feel like the majority of the work has been done. In a way it's true: setting the frame is a meticulous exercise that requires the team to align and agree. But only then does the real Event Design fun begin!

In our experience the ideas locked up in your Idea Quarantine can be the source of inspiration to kickstart your actual Design work. And so we would encourage you to clear your mind between the FRAME and DESIGN stages. The best way to do so is to actually plan the 2 steps on different days. Split design sessions over multiple shorter design sprints. Take a break, reflect, and come back to your design at a later time, or even another day.

TIP: Check out the online resource which includes a matrix and wiki of event formats and event ideas as well as reference books.

NOT HAVING ENOUGH IDEAS

Whilst you go through the process you may have forgotten to capture ideas that are popping up in the minds of your team members into the IDEA QUARANTINE. Trying to create them after switching from the linear process of CHANGE and FRAME to the creative process of DESIGN can be tough on the team. If the team gets stuck, use the LEAD methodology to assess your team's preferences; you might want to strategically expand the team at this stage. You can also try some exercises to get your team in the right mode: Take a walk with your team to get some fresh air—let yourselves become inspired by your environment, call out words of what you see, smell, feel, and think.

HAVING TOO MANY SCATTERED IDEAS

An overdose of ideas can clutter your thinking and make you lose focus. Ideas are nothing until they are brought to life. It's the beliefs that you are looking to alter that matter most. Try to cluster, combine, enrich, re-imagine, double, modify, blend, break, move, and fuse ideas. An overdose of ideas can be filtered by your team using the Idea Selection Matrix where you rank Feasibility versus Importance of each idea.

TIP: Filter your ideas using the Feasibility versus Importance Idea selection matrix.

FALLING IN LOVE WITH YOUR FIRST PROTOTYPE

It's easy to fall in love with your first ideas, seeing them come to life in 'your' prototype of choice. It is the facilitator's role to keep a neutral stance and check if, and how well, each prototype fits the checklist of the desired behaviour change.

TIP: Try the Event Simulator Facilitation Kit to guide your team through the process of Event Design and giving each team member a specific role.

FRIED BRAINS? PALATE CLEANSERS AND ADULT BEVERAGES

Event Design is fun, at least when done properly. Sometimes Stakeholder analysis and framing suck the life out of your team and you need to programme some palate cleansers (or adult beverages) to reignite the engines. Think of your Event Design sessions as an event you would like to attend. How can you make it matter? Design it with the end in mind. There are no limits to your creativity (well, at least not on paper).

DON'T LET THE OPINION OF ONE POLARISE YOUR GROUP INTO "GROUP THINK"

Event Design is not a solo sport; it's a team sport. Get inputs from each individual on paper and read them out loud. Celebrate opposing views and explore the boundaries of the possible when you hit a wall. Encourage a 'Yes, and…' approach to building on each others ideas and views instead of a 'Yes, but…' atmosphere.

TIP: Check out the 'Not Invented Here' resource.

TIP: Try the Event Simulator Facilitation Kit to guide your team through the process of Event Design and giving each team member a specific role.

TEAM REALLY HAPPY, BUT CAN'T SELL IT

Event Design may not be a concept, term, or practice that your organisation is familiar with. Its collaborative nature, its ability to engage teams, and its potential to create behaviour change for the good of the organisation may be a foreign concept to those who ultimately make company-wide decisions. Do not despair. Game-changers and innovators are always a bit disruptive and your being one may upset the status quo. If your decision maker has a fear of the unknown, ease them into the conversation with some examples as cited in this book, or print out some canvasses of events that have been designed with strong examples of behaviour change in mind. Tell the story of what this has done for other organisations and then show your willingness to take on the challenge based on a solid proven practice.

Investing 1% of the total event time on Event Design is the best time investment you can ask for. Spell out to the event owner the impact on the organisation by asking 'What If' questions: What if we just cancel this event if it's not worth our time? What if we were able to double the impact of the event, by design? Remember to apply what you have learned about influencing in Chapter 7 by catering to the leader's specific preference.

TIP: Print out and show examples of epic event designs on a single sheet of paper. Still not convincing enough? Try Dave Gray's 'Selling to the VP of No' worksheet; you will find it in the online resource for this handbook. Review the LEAD influence preference Dos & Don'ts cheat sheets in the online resources of this book.

WHAT SHOULD YOU DO AFTER YOU HAVE COMPLETED THE EVENT DESIGN?

The sense of achievement (and sigh of relief) when your preferred Event Design prototype has been approved is a moment to celebrate. However, failing to be diligent in supporting the team who put the event into action by following through on the event design may cause it to become diluted or even adjusted to a degree where the intent of the design and the desired effect of the behaviour change could get lost. Captains set out a course and get the crew to make adjustments based on the environment to reach the ultimate destination. Think carefully of your role and how you steer your ship. The Event Canvas is the compass for everyone on board.

TIP: Baseline your event on the Event Design you created and check back regularly checking delivery versus your Event Canvas.

BALLOONS
THINGS TO TRUST
& TRY FOR SUCCESS

TRUST THE TEAM
AND TRUST THE PROCESS

It's pretty incredible what teams can do if they are in the right mindset. Getting your team assembled, committed, and in the flow is probably your most challenging task. In chapters 4 and 7 you saw how to explore the best way to do so, and we encourage you to go back to those passages regularly when you start a new design session. Practice makes perfect. Trust your team and trust that the process works.

 TIP: If you are getting started and want the process and team to be guided every step of the way, give the Event Simulator Facilitation Kit™ a try. It's everything you need in a gamified box.

FACILITATION SKILLS, AND BEING
NEUTRAL AND CRITICAL TO THE
ACTUAL DESIGN INPUTS

It's tempting to get involved in the subject matter when you are facilitating a team, especially when it is your own team. We encourage you to practice, practice, practice, keeping a team on track and coaching them on process. You may also want to ask others who have developed the facilitation skills to take on the role so you can contribute to the content as a team member. Remember, you can lead from in front, or by supporting a team.

EVENT HISTORY = GOLD DUST

There are gems of knowledge and insight that can be mined by looking at the history and evolution of an event. Take some time to research and explore key behaviour changes of each event. Take note of the incremental steps taken and the time between events. Many clues will come to you. Some of our users have called this a post-mortem on the event, playing the detective to inspect the traces of what really happened. By assembling the clues and mapping them out in a historic timeline (use wallpaper and a timeline to make it visual) and having some eye witnesses involved, you will be amazed at what you didn't know that can be very relevant to future editions of the event.

NOT GETTING THE ATTENTION YOU NEED? THREATEN TO CANCEL THE EVENT!

If the event owner is not taking the event design process seriously, is not willing to allocate the time, the team, or the resources necessary, then see what happens if you threaten to cancel the event (hypothetically, that is). Creating this 'anti-problem' situation can be just the antidote to the toxic belief that Event Design time is a luxury and not a necessity. Amplify the pain of what happens (and what will certainly refrain from happening) when the event is no longer on the agenda for the event owner. It can be a brutally honest conversation to clear the air. Show your confidence in the value of events and your ability to design them.

Then, go to the intro of Chapter 4 to the Event Design time formula. Be persistent in claiming the right amount of Event Design time with the team of your choice and be ready to stand your ground. Be bold, be different, and go for it! It will lead to a completely new dynamic in your role and your organisation.

CREATE AN EVENT DESIGN 'WAR ROOM'

You read in Chapter 4 all about creating the right space in which to design your event. Maintaining a 'go-to' place for your team is a very effective tactic to keep your Event Design visible, actionable, and deliverable. In several instances we have pro-actively claimed an empty office space (there is always one

around) and put up the Event Wallpaper, and the kit of supporting canvasses and tools. It has been amazing to see the impact of claiming (temporary) space on the reaction of the team and the leadership. Even if this means overstepping your bounds, try it, be disruptive, and apologise later. And then send us a picture of your Event Design room.

WORK BIG, AMPLIFY THE PROBLEM

Working on poster-size Event Canvasses, equipping everyone with the right pens, sticky notes, and taking the design roles as outlined in the Event Simulator Facilitation kit seriously is the best way to ensure a good start. By amplifying the problem, you will get the right amount of attention and the team will be proud of contributing to cracking a 'big' design challenge. Additionally, your poster-size canvas in your event 'war room', will be reliable conversation starters with event owners and other Stakeholders.

TIP: Can't print poster size? Everything you need to equip your war room can be found online at www. edco.global/tools.

CAN'T TELL YOUR EVENT STORY IN 60 SECONDS? TRY 111 SECONDS

Sometimes doing recaps of the SAY & DO of the Stakeholder behaviours and of the final event narrative can be difficult to do in the moment. It is critical, we have found, to capture the outcomes of your finding as a team quickly after you have noted them down. What works well is to circle the key sticky notes with a coloured pen to highlight the story highlights to string the story together. Practice it and make a bit of a video competition out of it. Who can do the best narrative recap in 60 seconds (or as close as you can to 60 seconds)? A competitive element will always get a team on their feet.

 TIP: Start your Event Design session with the 111-second video clip about the Event Canvas.

PUT YOUR CANVASSES AT EYE-LEVEL IN A CHRONOLOGICAL ORDER

Designing on your feet is so much better than doing it sitting down. Tape the canvasses at eye-level (tape the poster size canvasses to the wall with masking tape) and make it a team exercise to get everyone warmed up. By standing up you will experience a much better energy and flow as a team, besides looking at the design challenge from the same angle. You will be amazed how much better Event Designs will be if you stand up as a team and face the problem 'head on'.

EVENT HORIZON

Having a hard time designing the very next event? Try designing one four years down the road.

Zooming out and designing the same event 4 or 5 years projected into the future can be a terrific way to get unstuck from incremental thinking. Strategic leaders and visionaries usually don't get particularly excited with short-term tactical improvements or alterations. Take your ambitions beyond the current event horizon and think 5 years ahead.

Design that future event with broad brush strokes first. This will allow you and your team to think freely without constraints of the timelines for the next edition. It will also attract the attention of your senior leaders if you ask them to imagine what an event would look like when their strategic 5-year objectives are achieved. By imagining what that event looks like and sketching it, you will have set an aim for where this event will go in the future.

From there you can now backcast your thinking of the number of events between now and then and what changes you want to apply to each of the events, starting with the first one next year. To get a visual of how that is done, check out the event horizon maps we use to support teams in this process.

> 'Life is like riding a bicycle. To keep your balance, you must keep moving.'

ALBERT EINSTEIN

THEORETICAL PHYSICIST

IT'S LIKE RIDING A BICYCLE

Event Design is like riding a bike. At the beginning it is very difficult and you might even think, 'Will I ever learn this?' However, after you master it, it is hard to imagine you ever found learning such skills difficult. You can watch all the videos and read all the books you want, but there is no other way to learn this then to get on the saddle.

PERMISSION VERSUS FORGIVENESS

You either start designing with your team and ask for forgiveness or ask for permission to do so ahead of time. In either case make sure you can get your event owner to spend 15 minutes of her valuable time to consider the prototypes you and your team have carefully crafted. You will be amazed at her ability to grasp the essence and her appreciation for the diligence you have shown in preparing these strategic alternatives for her to consider. Don't skip this step; it's your (and your team's) moment of glory to celebrate the power of Event Design.

WHAT WE'RE UP TO
NEXT

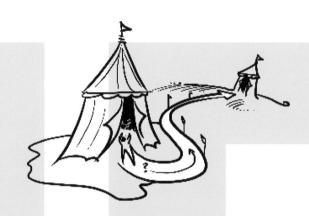

In this Event Design handbook we have focused on the process of systematically designing events with your team. Before we call on you to realise your very own behaviour change, we want to give you a glimpse into what we are working on next. Besides training and supporting teams to design events worth attending, we are building a gallery of Event Designs as an inspiration for event designers using the Event Canvas. As we gather more and more Event Designs we discover that every event has its own set of patterns and codes—this is Event DNA.

EVENT DNA—FINDING PATTERNS & CRACKING EVENT CODES

Over time, well-designed events establish patterns that become the very fabric of their success. They are the nodes of the organisational culture providing they have clear branding and are strategically aligned with the goals of the organisation. When you document and observe events systematically, you begin to notice patterns as if the events themselves reveal the DNA of the organisation.

Recognising the patterns behind your one-off event, or series of events, will allow you to design the unique interplay between the core Stakeholders and the context in which they operate. You can begin to see the patterns when you closely observe the behaviours of the Stakeholders as if you were an outsider.

We ask you to join us in our ongoing quest to code and decode events. Let's pretend for a moment you are an event anthropologist; your job is to piece together a story of an event based on information you cobble together during the event or after it has passed into history. The Event Canvas will be a powerful tool for you to evaluate, describe, and document any event from a position of observation. Documenting behaviours at an event can be done easily using a smartphone or a camera and taking photos or video snippets of every aspect in chronological order. The chain of events that you observe provides clues to the DNA of the event. Putting each photo or video in the context of the Event Canvas gives you the building blocks of the story of the event.

A SNEAK PEEK INTO WHAT'S NEXT

Each story of the event tells us something more about the patterns demonstrated by that event.

When studying events more closely, you will discover that each event has its own unique DNA.
These DNA patterns can be evaluated on various levels and considered to have various natures. If you are curious to find out more, check out the white-paper with our preliminary observations of the findings, and contribute your insights, experiences, and canvases to the Event Design community, and help develop the next frontier of Event Design.

We invite you to share your event designs with us. Your contributions will allow everyone to benefit from understanding events better. So we can start analysing the DNA of successful events and share our findings in the next editions of this publication.

TIP: Contribute to the Event Design Gallery by submitting your Event Designs and share using #EventCanvas.

TIME FOR ACTION, IT'S YOUR TURN!

Last but not least it's your time to apply what you have read in this book. The next chapter will give you 7 things you can do next to get started as well as a full overview in a glossary of the Event Language.

TRINA SHARP

EVENT MANAGER, POINT B

'The Event Design process is crucial to a successful event. The better it is understood, the more likely a stakeholder will buy in. The Event Design Certificate program gives you the background you need to make it possible for you to be the event leader and possess the skills necessary to lead your team to a successful event!'

TED MOONEY

SENIOR DIRECTOR OF MEMBERSHIP AND SERVICES, INTERNET SOCIETY

'The Event Canvas process allows team innovation to emerge like no other process I've experienced. The event design solutions are imaginative, engaging, provocative, and they produce results. It should be embraced not just by meeting planners, but business leaders who want real bottom-line impact from their event investment.'

09.

'Improve our world, one event at a time!'

YOUR TURN

TO DI

CHAPTER 09

Check out
online resources

Share your learnings
on social media

Select Event
to (re-)design

**www.eventcanvas.org
/resources**

#EventCanvas

**Discuss your
Event Delta**

EDC

Join the EventCanvas
Community

Event Design
Training options

Set up your Event
Design Space

Get your team
on board

**Share your
Event Designs**

**Event Design
Certificate**

**Event Simulator
Facilitation Kit**

**make
Event Design Time**

The last part of this book is dedicated to an Event Design Glossary of the terminology and concepts you have read and seen in this handbook.
Your biggest asset in successfully deploying what you have read here is your taking action. We hope to help you create a common visual language that will help make the process of Event Design a clear one, ready for the future of collaborative events all over the world.

In time we hope this will also allow you to contribute to the quality and openness of Event Design thinking, to elevate the valuation of Event Design in professional circles, and to elevate the status of your event and your designing of it.

Last but not least, remember that the only way your reading of this book can create value is if it actually changes your behaviour. You have to 'SAY & DO' something. Your actions will give us the energy and delight to continue our quest to create a common visual language for Event Design.

To us it's critical to see 'proof' of this behaviour change. Will you help us by taking one or all of the following actions? What happens next is in your hands.

AMANDA LARSON

MARKETING DIRECTOR, CLAREITY SECURITY

'The Event Design Certificate program provides a great oversight to event planning and forces event professionals to view events differently. I think this approach creates a universal language that all event professionals can comprehend and understand. A perfect template to describe the importance of event design to others – stakeholders, vendors, bosses, etc.'

EVENT DESIGN
GLOSSARY

Braiding Point: The point in the process when those that have a stake in the Event Design project actually start.

Canvas Thinking: Using visual models to reduce or manage complexity and to create shared mental models.

Canvas Tool: A one-page template summary used to reduce complexity in business, life, or society.

Circus Tent: A visual metaphor in this book used to represent an event.

Event: Any gathering of two or more people or groups of people.

Empathy Map: A visual-thinking tool on a single piece of paper that allows a team to analyse and articulate the sensory perceptions, feelings, behaviours,and pains and gains of a specific Stakeholder; originally developed by Dave Gray at Xplane.com.

Empathy Mapping: The process of analysing a Stakeholder's perspective using an Empathy Map.

Event Canvas™: A visual-thinking tool on a single piece of paper that allows people to articulate how an event creates value. The Event Canvas was developed by Roel Frissen and Ruud Janssen and can be studied further at eventcanvas.org. It has 14 specific elements:

01 Entering Behaviour: What a Stakeholder says and does prior to the event

02 Pains: Issues and situations that make the Stakeholder feel negative or fearful.

03 Expectations: The assumption or supposition of what the event will be like. They are based on previous experiences, word-of-mouth, social media, and marketing messages.

04 Exiting Behaviour: What a Stakeholder says and does as a result of having participated in the event.

05 Gains: What the Stakeholder dreams about or aspires to.

06 Satisfaction: The degree to which EXPECTATIONS have been met or exceeded, or to which the event has fallen short. This is what someone would tell others about the event after it has taken place.

07 Commitment: The (in)tangible investment the Stakeholder makes in time and effort.

08 Return: What the Stakeholder wants to obtain as a result of having attended the event.

09 Cost: The fixed and variable expenses associated with the event for a specific Stakeholder.

10 Revenue: The financial income or yield of the event in monetary terms of the event for a specific Stakeholder.

11 Jobs to be Done: Functional, social, or emotional tasks that need doing; basic needs the Stakeholder is trying to satisfy.

12 Promise: The 'gift' that attracts Stakeholders to an event; it presents the basic input for the marketing message. A good PROMISE is concise: in our exercises we ask people to write it as a 140-character tweet; ideally it can be the same for all Stakeholders. In this way it is to the event what a tagline is for a movie.

13 Experience Journey: The chronological interactions someone has before, during, and after an event. The EXPERIENCE JOURNEY shapes the intended change of behaviour with specific moments.

14 Instructional Design: The way in which the event enables the Stakeholder to learn specific skills, acquire knowledge, or develop a desired attitude. This also involves the way in which people get to know each other on a personal level as a result of having attended the event.

Event Delta: The intended change in behaviour of the key Stakeholders as a result of attending an event.

Event Design: The process of articulating change, setting the boundaries, and prototyping your event using design thinking and doing.

Event Design Room: A dedicated space with ample wall space where a team can design events.

Event Design Team: A motivated team that is ready (with both time and space) to innovate their event.

Event Narrative: the story of the event from entry to exit of the event.

Idea Quarantine: A place to retain otherwise orphan ideas that come up during the design process, usually on a separate flip chart. The ideas remain isolation until late in the DESIGN stage of the Event Canvas methodology.

LEAD Stakeholder Influencer Instrument: A methodology to identify the specific preferences of team members that allows you to better understand the approach and role of team members in the Event Design process; A structured approach to positively influence a Stakeholder by catering to their personal preference as an individual.

Overarching Aim: An overarching general statement of the direction where a team needs to go and what it wants to achieve. It is a direction-finding statement without any specific detail.

Prototype: A rough sample of what the Event Design could look like. Multiple prototypes side-by-side make it more possible to choose the one that will likely work best.

Stakeholder: A person or group of people with an interest or concern in an Event. They choose to create or be part of an event because it is more important to them to participate than to not.

Stakeholder Alignment Canvas: A visual-thinking tool on a single piece of paper that allows users to long-list Stakeholders, rank them, and arrange them in a matrix with 2 axes: one for power and the other for level of interest. Ultimately, the Stakeholder Alignment Canvas allows users to align a team to the appropriate Stakeholders to design for, and to identify the Overarching Aim. The Stakeholder Alignment Canvas was developed by David Bancroft Turner, Roel Frissen, Ruud Janssen, and Dennis Luijer.

REFERENCES

Dave Gray, Sunni Brown, and James Macafuno. *Gamestorming*.
O'Reilly Media Inc. 2010.

Osterwalder, Alexander, and Pigneur, Yves, Smith, Alan, et. al.
Business Model Generation. Wiley. 2010,

Phillips J., Breining, M. Theresa, and Phillips, Patricia Pullman.
Return on Investment in Meetings & Events. Elsevier Inc. 2008.

Stickdorn, Marc, and Schneider, Marc, et.al.
This is Service Design Thinking. BIS Publishers. 2010.

Solaris, Julius, *Event Manager Blog*
http://www.eventmanagerblog.com/

Thomas, Wayne, and Bancroft-Turner, David.
LEAD and Stakeholder Influencing Instrument.
MatrixTC.com

Watkins, Alan, *The Secret Science of Brilliant Leadership*.
Meeting Professionals International European Meetings & Events
Conference #EMEC 2015, Krakow, Poland. 2015.

ACKNOWLEDGEMENTS
& SPECIAL THANKS

HOW EVENTS CAN LEAD TO INITIATIVES
What serendipitous series of events led to the creation of this book?

Curiously enough, events were the root cause of the creation of this Event Design handbook. Authors Ruud Janssen and Roel Frissen's volunteer leadership roles—initially in Meeting Professionals International (MPI) in the Netherlands, and later with the International Board of Directors, and later as consultants—brought us together to work on myriad projects. We were particularly inspired by the application of the Business Model Canvas at a MPI International Board of Director's meeting just prior to the World Education Congress in Vancouver, Canada, in 2010, which included meeting it's creator Alex Osterwalder. This experience sparked a series of ideas on how visual and design thinking could shift the status quo of events.

Thinking led to doing, and we developed a first prototype of what later became the Event Canvas just prior to participating in the Business Design Summit in 2013 in Berlin. The 'Rise of the Tool-smiths' as called for by Alex Osterwalder and his team and a workation with them after at that event became the beginning of an exciting journey across the globe that tried and tested the Event Design methodology that we present in this book.

A key component that we felt was missing from the Event Design equation was drawing out change. This led us, as the creators of the Event Canvas, to meet

Dennis Luijer, whose former company Jam Visual Thinking was involved in the creation of the visuals within the Business Model Canvas. An incubator in January 2014, with a number of pioneers and event industry innovators laid the foundation for the validation of the Event Canvas. And Dennis' fascination for drawing out the change of ENTRY and EXIT BEHAVIOURS connected him to the cause.

The development of the Event Canvas has since enabled us to work with a large diversity of teams, cultures, and organisations who embrace the opportunity of designing better events.

Creating a common language can only be done if the way it is done is open and inclusive. From the beginning, we have decided to share the Event Canvas under a creative commons 4.0 license in order to facilitate its distribution and adoption across the globe. Since it's launch on 14 February, 2014, the Event Canvas has been translated by volunteers into multiple languages including Simplified Mandarin Chinese, German, French, Russian, Portuguese, and Dutch, with more to follow.

We've been inspired by the energy, dedication, and eagerness of teams to question and challenge their current thinking and to try the methodology. This willingness of teams to cut new trails has led us to launch training programmes, and since 2015, to offer Event Design Certificate programmes with universities in multiple continents.

Driven by the needs of Event Canvas users, we were encouraged to first develop hands-on instruction for the 'how to' design events, which is now available as the Event Simulator Facilitation Kit^sm. This handbook was subsequently written to inspire and equip you as users with the necessary background, application, and case study insights to spur you and your teams to action.

This book would not have been possible if it were not for the countless individuals (you know who you are as you are reading this) who contributed to its creation. First of all, we'd like to acknowledge our Dads and Moms who nurtured us to be curious of our surroundings and to appreciate what really matters in life. Also, we thank our dear wives and children, who have endured our endless days of travel and hours online to get to where we are. Their support means the world to us.

Last but not least, we would like to express our gratitude to the people who believe in what we do and have been instrumental in moving us to where we are:

Thanks to our contributors Julius Solaris, David Bancroft-Turner, and Dave Gray for their wit and willingness to share generously; to our driven publisher, Bionda Dias at BIS Publishing in Amsterdam; the keen eye of the designer of this book, Cristel Lit, who endured our evolving design ideas and inked them onto the paper; our editor and contributing co-author John Loughlin, who word-smithed our thinking into legible text with his sharp pen. We owe a lot to our practitioners and change-makers at the organisations who have championed the process internally, including FERMA, MED-EL, Achmea, Internet Society, United Nations, International Olympic Committee, and all those who followed.

And we would like to show our appreciation to individuals who have helped us in their own ways; we are deeply indebted:

THANK YOU

Alan Smith
Alex Osterwalder
Alfred Keijzer
Alissa Hurley
Amanda Armstrong
Amanda Larson
Amber Herrewijn
Ambre Vergy
Amy Wang
Andreas Laube
Anna Johansson
Annaliza Laxamana
Annette Gregg
Anthony Back
Babs Nijdam
Benoit Hurel
Brahima Sanou
Carl Winston
Cecilia Ljunglöf
Christian Mutschlechner
Damian Hutt
David Kliman
Debbie Fox
Deborah Sexton
Elling Hamso
Elsa Luijer
Emilia Åström
Eric de Groot
Florence Bindelle
Gerrit Jessen

Gwynne Janssen
Han-Maurits Schaapveld
Jeannell Kolkman
Jennifer Fischer-Belmonte
Joe Pine
Joyce Dogniez
Julie Neuveu
Karine Mourey
Kasey Connors
Kathy Brown
Kemal Huseinovic
Kevin Hinton
Laura Ditiere
Lisa Halmschlager
Lykle de Vries
Maarten Vanneste
Mariano Suarez-Battan
Marleen Herzlieb
Marti Winer
Martin Alline
Martin van Keken
Matthias Spacke
Mike van der Vijver
Miranda van Brück
Mohamed Ba
Monika Birkle
Myriam Gómez
Nicole Armstrong
Panos Tzivanidis
Paul Van Deventer

Pauline Meslet
Peter Sonderegger
Petra Bauer-Zwinz
Pierre Sonigo
Renita Carter
Roberta Dias
Sabine Bonora
Samme Allen
Sjoerd Weikamp
Sofie Maddens
Stephanie Arehart
Stephanie Dathe
Sue Gordon
Suzan Franssen
Ted Mooney
Terri Breining
Terri Crovato
Tony Fundaro
Trina Sharp
Vera Kurpershoek
Victor Nyendorff
Vivi Henao
Willemijn Westra
Yulia Boytsova

And finally, thank YOU, the reader
of this handbook (+ the person to
whom you will suggest it).

MEET
THE AUTHORS

ROEL FRISSEN
@roelfrissen

Roel is entrepreneur, speaker, facilitator and event designer for corporations and associations. On a quest to create a common and visual language to ease the conversation between Event Planner and Event Owner, he created together with Ruud Janssen the Event Canvas™. Roel is the co-founder of Event Design Collective and Event Model Generation -the event design consulting & training firm.

RUUD JANSSEN
@ruudwjanssen

Ruud is an international speaker, facilitator and designer of high stakes conferences & events. He helps organisations innovate by thinking differently based on functional, social and technological advancements using business and event model innovation. He created the Event Canvas™ with Roel Frissen to enable teams to systematically design events that matter. Ruud is is the co-founder of Event Design Collective and Event Model Generation -the event design consulting & training firm.

DENNIS LUIJER
@visiblethinking

Visual Change Master Dennis believes in making thoughts visible by drawing them out into reality. His role in visualising how events create value, brings the narrative and long term perspective to life. As co-founder of the Event Design Collective he works constantly to improve & design the visual tooling that helps to ensure great Event Design. As a visual work space consultant he helps companies to claim the space and train people to make their challenges visible by drawing them out.

VISIT

www.eventcanvas.org

to find out more about

Event Design and the Event Canvas